Elements of Distribution

A textbook for the Business and Technician Education Council
General Award Course

R. H. Robertshaw and J. R. Willans
Lecturers in the Distributive Trades in the
Business Studies Department, Huddersfield Technical College

POLYTECH PUBLISHERS LTD STOCKPORT

First published 1979
Reprinted March 1983
Revised Edition 1984

Set in 10 pt Times series by
Bury Phototypesetting Limited, Peel Mills, Bury, Lancashire
and printed in Great Britain by
Ashworths Print Services, Peel Mills, Bury, Lancashire

Contents

Preface

This book is intended to help those people who have embarked on a career in distribution, or those who are following a course which is preparing them for such a career.

We believe the book meets the needs of students following the B/TEC General and other basic courses. Although written with the B/TEC General objectives in mind we have included additional relevant material. This will assist the student in acquiring a better understanding of the basic processes involved in the distributive industry. The book follows a logical pattern of development but it is not our intention to impose this as the only possible teaching sequence.

Our sincere thanks are due to the many people who have assisted us in the preparation of the book. Special mention is due to:—

Alan Taylor for his work as editor and adviser;

Janet Payne whose illustrations have brought both humour and variety to the text. These we hope will serve as invaluable reminders to the student.

As with other books in this series there is a teachers manual which contains outline answers to the exercises, suggestions for additional assignments and guidance on assessment.

We have taken the opportunity to revise and update the text in line with B/TEC amendments.

R.H.R.
J.R.W.
March 1984

Acknowledgements

We would like to acknowledge the assistance given by:-

H.M.S.O.
(for permission to reproduce statistical tables);

Midland Bank Ltd
(for permission to reproduce the illustration of a cheque and bankers card).

Chapter 1

Introduction to Distribution

At the end of this chapter you should be able to explain the background to the development of distribution in our society.

In particular this means being able to:-

(A) **Define distribution.**

(B) **Describe self sufficiency.**

(C) **Define barter.**

(D) **Describe the disadvantages of barter.**

(E) **Identify the changes which caused the growth in distribution.**

1.1 *What is distribution?*

Distribution has many meanings but a simple definition would have to include the idea of getting goods and services to people who want them and who can pay for them. Subsequent chapters will expand upon this basic idea.

Distribution = provision of goods and services when needed, to those who require them.

It is not the function of distribution to create these goods and services. Distribution channels these goods and services from, say, industry represented by a shoe factory to the customer.

1.2 *Self sufficiency*

Early man was able to satisfy his own material needs, which were then food, shelter and warmth. Each man or family grouping provided these things for themselves by hunting, fishing and primitive agriculture. They looked after themselves relying on nobody outside the group to provide them with anything. This is known as self sufficiency.

1.3 *Barter*

As man developed and settled down in one place, he began to acquire certain skills which resulted in some cases in the creation of surplus goods.

A farmer might have more grain than he needed whilst someone else might have some surplus animal skins. The obvious way for each to dispose of the surplus was to swap the grain for the animal skins, assuming each wanted what the other had to offer. This swapping of one item for another is known as "barter". It is the earliest form of distribution.

Barter is still used today, e.g. schoolboys swapping comics, neighbours exchanging gardening produce with each other.

It is also found in business, where a would-be customer cannot pay in an acceptable form of money. Some countries are short of money to buy foreign goods, so they pay for these imports by a system of barter, e.g. defence equipment is exchanged for oil.

Ford, the car manufacturer, maintains an organisation whose function is to arrange barter deals for Ford products and then to arrange the sale, for cash, of the bartered goods obtained.

Barter has, however, two disadvantages:-

(a) *Double co-incidence of wants is necessary* — each person must want what the other has to offer, e.g. a fisherman with surplus fish may wish to exchange (or barter) them for pots, but if the potter does not want fish, then trade cannot take place.

(b) *Valuing goods* — how much of one thing is something else worth? e.g. how many fish for a pot? This is sometimes called the "rate of exchange".

These two disadvantages led to the introduction of money which was necessary for the development of distribution.

1.4 *Exercise 1*

1 What is distribution?

2 Define in your own words the term self sufficiency.

3 What were the basic needs of early man?

4 Define barter giving one example.

5 What are the two drawbacks of barter?

1.5 *Money*

Money fulfils a number of functions, two of which are particularly important to the distributive industry.

(a) *As a measure of value* — goods and services can be valued in money terms, e.g. a chair may be valued at £50 and a table at £200. Therefore the table is worth four chairs, or put another way, the rate of exchange is four chairs for a table. All goods and services can be given a money value, thus enabling people to obtain the best possible benefits from their work.

(b) *As a medium of exchange* — money overcomes the difficulty of barter in terms of the double co-incidence of wants as money is acceptable in exchange for all goods and services. The shopkeeper will accept money in exchange for his stock knowing that others will accept this money in exchange for the things the shopkeeper requires.

Just imagine the difficulties that would occur if your store refused to accept money: how would it continue to trade? Yet legally they could do so. To be absolutely sure of acceptance money must be "legal tender", that is money which the law requires you to accept as payment. Legal tender consists of Bank of England notes and £1 coins in any amount, up to £10 in 20p or 50p pieces, £5 in 10p and/or 5p coins, and 20p in copper coins, but in practice shops would accept payment in coins above these amounts since failure to do so may result in losing the sale. Additionally, the store may be short of change.

1.6 Early forms of distribution

The earliest organised forms of distribution were the market place and the pedlar.

(a) *The market*. Occurs where buyers and sellers meet to trade. Nowadays with modern communications, e.g. telex and telephone, face to face contact is not necessary. Buyer and seller can, in fact, be several thousand miles apart.

Historically, markets occurred at a regular fixed time, such as Whitsuntide or on a particular day. Location was also fixed. Market days in market squares are a continuation of this tradition, often these markets were accompanied by side shows and entertainers.

Medieval Market

4

(b) *The pedlar.* In the past those who could not get to a market may, on occasions, have been visited by a pedlar. He would travel from one place to another selling small trinkets and household necessities. Pedlars also brought news of the outside world to small isolated communities. Both these forms of distribution mainly served farming communities whose needs were simple. Small numbers of shops existed in the towns to meet the requirements of the limited number of people who then lived there. Major changes in the distribution system in this country took place when people started working in towns and factories rather than on the land.

1.7 *The reasons for the growth of the distribution industry.*

(a) Some two hundred years ago Britain experienced what has been called "the industrial revolution". This was a gradual change to a situation where the majority of workers were employed in manufacturing industry, in some way or other.

The spread of industrialisation created the conditions necessary for a rapid growth in the size and complexity of the distribution network.

(b) The changes which occurred were:-

(i) The growth of specialisation and the division of labour. This meant that people were encouraged to develop, to a high level, a limited number of skills. Thus they became more dependent on others to provide them with many of the things which earlier generations provided for themselves. A more extensive distribution system was necessary to provide them with those goods and services.

(ii) Those who worked on the land received much of their wages in kind, i.e. food and accommodation were supplied by the farm. They would thus be paid only a very small part of their wages in cash. When the majority of people started working in factories, they had to spend money on food, accommodation and other goods and services. The extra money and need for these goods and services encouraged the growth and development of distribution.

(iii) More employment in factories encouraged people to leave the land, so increasing the population of many towns and cities. These people had to be fed, clothed and provided with various goods and services.

(iv) Increased affluence caused by factories providing more and more jobs which eventually started paying improved wages to workers. Thus the demand for goods and services provided by shops increased. Britain as a relatively well off country is able to support a large distribution network.

1.8 *Distribution — an ever changing industry*

Distribution has evolved from simple barter by individuals to a complex large scale industry in order to meet the changing needs of people.

Distribution is not static, it is always changing to meet new needs as and when they arise viz

(a) the need for 'one stop' shopping, buying everything inside one store, for people whose shopping time is limited, and where parking facilities are restricted;

(b) the development of various forms of credit to help people buy expensive goods; (see 15.2)

(c) developing specialist shops to meet new needs, e.g. dry cleaning, hi-fi, homebrewing and health foods. Of one thing we can be fairly certain, the distribution system of today will undergo major changes in the future.

1.9 *Exercise 2*

1 How did money overcome the drawbacks of barter?

2 Define legal tender.

3 What is a market?

4 Give two reasons for the growth of distribution.

5 Illustrate how distribution has developed to meet changing needs.

1.10 **Assignments**

1 Prepare a chart to show how four people, none of whom initially can barter, may arrange a barter deal between themselves.

2 List ten products or services a factory or office worker might need, but is not able to provide for himself, and which the distribution system supplies. Additionally, list five goods or services he could, if he wished, provide for himself.

6

Chapter 2

The Role and Importance of Distribution in Society

At the end of this chapter you should be able to identify the role and importance of distribution in society.

In particular this means being able to:-

(A) List the 'five rights'.

(B) Define each of these 'rights'.

(C) State examples of these 'rights'.

(D) State the criteria used to judge the importance of distribution.

(E) Explain each of these criteria.

2.1 *The role of distribution in society*

Distribution has not one role but several. These can perhaps be most easily illustrated in terms of what have been described as the 'five rights'.

Providing the 'right' goods

At the 'right' time;

At the 'right' price;

Of the 'right' quantity;

In the 'right' place;

Any more late deliveries and I'll buy Japanese

2.2   (a) *The 'right' goods — the provision of goods and services*

Ask most people what shops do and they are likely to reply 'sell things'. By this they mean shops provide a wide variety of goods and services to potential customers.

Think of some of the stores in just one of the main shopping streets in your town and the variety of things that they sell — i.e. food items, clothes, leisure goods, furniture, medical products. Indeed just one store, a large supermarket or department store (about which, more later) stocks several thousand different items. Harrods, the famous London department stores had as its telegraphic address 'Everything' London.

Shops sell not only different items, but the same item in various sizes, colours, styles and makes, e.g. television sets and furniture, to give the customer even more choice.

Furthermore, shops provide goods which they believe their customers will be interested in buying. If they do not, then they will not make sales and risk going out of business.

The customer, and now the law, require goods and services to be of an acceptable standard. Failure to maintain these standards can result in lost sales and the possibility of legal action.

Many retailers are now more actively engaged in quality control, i.e. making sure that the goods they offer for sale are of an acceptable quality and of a certain standard.

Quality control is too large a subject to be dealt with at this stage. However, you should remember that quality control involves:-

(i)   checking goods delivered for damage or sub-standard goods;

(ii) checking packaging for damage;

(iii) ensuring goods are sold before they become unfit for sale;

(iv) ensuring the goods are properly and carefully handled;

(v) dealing only with reputable suppliers;

(vi) ensuring sub-standard goods are not sold;

Some stores are so successful at quality control that they get a reputation for selling high quality goods e.g. Marks & Spencers.

As well as improving sales and the business's image, ensuring goods are of the right quality is necessary in view of the growth of the number of laws designed to protect the customer, e.g. Sale of Goods Act 1979 and Unfair Contract Terms Act 1977.

Under the law the retailer can be heavily fined for selling sub-standard goods, or in certain circumstances can even be sent to prison.

(b) *The 'right' time — providing goods and services when they are needed.*

Through shops and other distribution outlets e.g. vending machines or mail order, the customer can obtain the goods and services he wants when he wants them. Most goods are available at anytime the customer wants them.

For other items demand tends to be seasonal or lasts for a short time, e.g. Easter eggs, Christmas stock and fireworks. The distribution system ensures that when the customer wants goods and services, they are available, even if this requires the retailers placing orders months in advance. This often calls for skill on the part of the retailer in forecasting what and how much he should order in advance.

If he orders too little, he loses sales. If he orders too much of any item(s) he might be left with stock which he cannot sell, especially if he deals in merchandise which is subject to fashion, e.g. teenage clothes, or a fad, e.g. skateboards.

We sometimes take this availability of goods for granted. Without an efficient distribution system there would be shortages. As it is the products of many parts of the world are available to us when we want them. They are ordered, paid for, and stored for us until we, the customers, decide we want them.

(c) *The 'right' price — providing goods and services at the right price*

Shops need to provide goods and services at a price which their customers can afford and are prepared to pay. Some shops charge more than others, but this is because they —

(i)   sell better quality goods, e.g. 100% wool carpets or

(ii) have higher costs, e.g. pay more rates or

(iii) sell fewer goods, e.g. the corner shop is usually more expensive than the supermarket because it deals in smaller quantities than the large store.

If goods are priced too highly then sales will drop, e.g. during 1976 the retail price of coffee doubled causing many people to switch to tea or a coffee/chicory mixture.

Until quite recently few prices were fixed. Often the price was decided between the buyer and seller — each trying to get the best price. A department store in Paris (Bon Marché) and the Quakers in this country are credited with the introduction of the idea of a fair fixed price.

Many manufacturers sought to enforce the price at which their goods could be sold by withholding supplies or by taking legal action. In 1964 the law was changed so that only certain goods had to be sold at a price set by the manufacturers. Virtually all prices now are recommended prices. (Resale Prices Acts 1964 and 1976).

(d) *The 'right' quantity*

Often the quantity in which the goods are available is very important to certain people:-

(i) Often pensioners and others on low incomes do not have the money to buy goods in anything but the smallest quantity available. Their budgets will not allow them to buy large or economy sizes. Hence they may often pay a high price in relation to the quantity bought.

(ii) Those who buy in bulk — Freezer owners buy in bulk to save money and shopping time. Shopping can be done once a month. This group of people tend to 'stock up' their freezers and other storage facilities from stores which cater for this type of customer.

(e) *The 'right' place — goods and services and hence shops need to be located at places convenient for the customers*

This usually means shopping centres and precincts from which motor traffic is banned, and corner shops in residential areas. Distribution is very competitive and if a store is inconveniently situated then potential customers will go elsewhere.

Sometimes though a convenient location can cease to be so. This occurs when a new road is built or some development such as a new bus station or the demolition of surrounding property occurs.

Some outlets do not need to be located inside a large population area or town centre, e.g. hypermarkets, but what they do need are good communications facilities, especially roads.

Finally, for some people it is necessary for the shops to come to them. This is particularly the case with the aged, the infirm and the housebound. For this additional convenience people pay in the form of a reduced choice of goods and generally higher prices.

2.3 Exercise 1

1 List the five 'rights' which a retailer should provide.

2 Retailers provide choice. Explain this statement.

3 Give four examples of seasonal goods. What special problems arise through stocking these goods?

4 Why might one retailer charge more for a product than another? Illustrate your answer by means of suitable examples.

5 Suggest why prices charged by travelling shops may be higher than those charged by other types of shops.

2.4 Importance of distribution

Distribution workers generally are regarded as belonging to an industry in which the workers are not highly paid when compared with workers in some other industries, despite the fact that it makes a number of major contributions to our society viz

(a) *Quality of life*

Without the choice provided by retailers and other sectors of distribution, the quality of life would be less than it is. Obtaining a supply of the reduced amount of goods and services which would be available if there were no organised system of distribution would be more time consuming than it is now. Shortages of goods would result in queueing. Furthermore, if there were no shops or the distribution system which supplied them, how and where would you obtain what you require?

(b) *Enables specialisation to take place*

In all but the most primitive economies specialisation takes place (our potter, fisherman, baker and hunter in the previous chapter are 'specialists'). It is one of the main causes of economic growth. Specialisation occurs where an individual or area concentrates on the provision of a particular good or service. For example, should you go into hospital with an eye disease, you would be seen by an eye 'specialist', someone who concentrates on (specialises in) treating diseases of the eyes. Many people in many other occupations are specialists in this sense, e.g. television repairman who specialises in servicing/repairing televisions, window dressers, accountants, and so on.

You may become a specialist in selling a particular type of merchandise, e.g. furniture, as a specialist furniture salesman. You would specialise by acquiring a good knowledge of the product (see 13.5), i.e. what furniture is made of, characteristics, prices and the like. As a specialist, people would come to you for advice when buying furniture.

Specialisation also occurs geographically. An area or country specialises in producing a particular good or service, e.g. Brazil with coffee and Sheffield with cutlery.

Specialisation results in a wider range of goods and services being produced. Often fewer resources are used (hence lower prices) and the goods are of a higher quality than would be the case if it did not operate.

The doctor knows he can satisfy all his needs for goods and services created by other specialists through the distributive system. He is able to concentrate on, and develop, his medical skills to the benefit of society.

(c) *Employment*

The industry provides over two million jobs. Only the public services and engineering employ more people.

Distribution provides many part-time jobs for those who (perhaps because of family commitments) can only work part-time. Without distribution, employment opportunities of this type would be much more limited.

It provides a vast range of employment opportunities from merchandising to managerial posts at the most demanding levels.

(d) *Foreign exchange*

Many stores particularly those in areas visited by large numbers of foreign tourists, e.g. Central London, sell considerable quantities of goods to foreigners, thereby earning for themselves, and the country millions of £'s in foreign currency. Some of these stores employ staff who can speak foreign languages.

(e) *Taxation*

The industry acts as an (unpaid) collector of taxes. The Government levies tax and excise duties on a large number of goods and services. These are known as indirect taxes. When a store sells such an item, it is collecting both the price of the item and the tax on it. Taxes and excise duties which retailers help collect include:-

(i) Value Added Tax (VAT);

(ii) Excise duties on tobacco and alcohol;

(iii) Duty on petrol;

Excise duties are paid by the manufacturer. He then includes this in the price charged to the retailer, who in turn passes this charge on to his customers.

Without the help of the industry, reluctant though it may sometimes be, the cost of collecting taxes would be higher than it is.

Retailers also pay tax on their profits.

(f) *Rates*

Shops, warehouses and other premises used for distribution purposes pay rates to the local authority. This may range from a few hundred pounds for a small shop in a low rate area to over £1 million for a large store in the centre of a big city.

Without this substantial income from the large number of distribution premises, the local authorities would possibly have to charge more for household rates and/or provide fewer services and amenities.

2.5 *Added value*

The role of distribution involves satisfying the needs of its customers by having the right goods of the right quantity and right price in the right place at the right time. In doing this the industry adds value to the goods and services it offers. An umbrella may cost £4 to make but be sold for £8. The extra £4 is the cost of providing the customer with these 'five rights'. After all, a £4 umbrella made in Scotland last month and still held in store there is no use today to a potential customer walking round London in the pouring rain!

Distribution is a very important industry no matter what criteria are used to measure its importance, e.g. economic or employment possibilities. Without distribution we would all lead very much poorer lives in every sense of the word.

12

2.6 *Exercise 2*

1   How does distribution encourage specialisation?

2   Why did some stores in Newcastle-upon-Tyne encourage their staff to take basic courses in Norwegian?

3   Why might a local authority be keen on a new shopping centre being built in its area?

4   Name four items sold on which a tax or duty is paid and state the tax or duty levied.

5   Using an example of your own choosing, show how distribution adds value to that item.

2.7 **Assignments**

1   Select any shop you wish and show how it fulfils the role of distribution. Use the 'five rights' as the basis of your answer.

2   List ten different jobs which occur in distribution, indicating which may be suitable for those seeking part-time employment.

Chapter 3

Social Effects

At the end of this chapter you should be able to describe how distribution affects modern life. **In particular this means being able to:-**

(A) **Identify the effects of distribution on individuals.**

(B) **List the possible ways in which the physical distribution of goods can affect modern life.**

(C) **Describe how distribution affects the development of town centres.**

3.1 *Scope of effects*

Distribution is one industry which affects the lives of us all. In addition to those aspects mentioned in earlier units, namely, the provision of goods and services and other economic aspects e.g. the provision of employment, distribution affects us in other ways. These can for convenience be grouped into:-

(a) Effects on individuals.

(b) Environmental effects.

3.2 *Effects on individuals*

(a) *Social*

Most people like to meet other people, to talk to them and to get to know them. Distribution provides many opportunities for such meetings, especially in small retail stores.

Some people seek shop work because of this, indeed some advertisements for sales staff stress this point. As sales assistants you have more opportunities than most to meet and help people.

To many people shopping is something of a social occasion e.g. old age pensioners and mothers with very young children. A visit to the shops may be socially very important. It perhaps offers the chance of meeting friends and neighbours who are also out shopping. This has been put forward as one reason for the continued existence of the small corner shop despite competition from supermarkets and others.

(b) *Additional services*

Some stores, mainly the large ones, provide limited banking services e.g. for cashing cheques. This can be very useful to people who cannot get to the bank. Some stores have A.T.M.'s (Automatic Telling Machines) installed.

(c) *Convenience shopping*

In order to meet the needs of large sections of society, who for a variety of reasons have limited opportunities to shop e.g. the millions of working wives. Distribution has evolved in the following ways:-

(i) Late night shopping — some stores have one or more late closing nights when they may stay open until 8 o'clock or later. This enables people who cannot shop at any other time to do so, it also provides the opportunity for family shopping expenditions.

(ii) Convenience foods — An increasing number and variety of food items are being sold which require little or no preparation such as instant mashed potatoes, tea bags and frozen foods.

(d) *Adverse effects*

It can be argued that the modern distribution industry may cause harm to certain individuals by:-

(i) Encouraging people to steal — A store tries to display its merchandise in such ways as to encourage sales. In doing so it may tempt some people to steal especially if goods are on open display and customers serve themselves. See 17.4 and 13.4.

Many people when charged with stealing from a shop explain that
a) They were tempted by the attractive way in which the goods were displayed and the ease with which they could be picked up.
b) They fully intended to pay but forgot to do so, had there been a sales assistant there at the time they would most certainly have paid.

The extent to which modern retailing techniques encourage/tempt people to steal is arguable. In some instances their use must have helped to tempt customers.

(ii) Encouraging people to buy things they really don't need or cannot afford — How true this may be is open to argument, though it must be true in some cases because of the relative availability of credit. People, though, must feel some need for a good or service before they will buy it.

Whether or not he or she can afford it, is for the buyer alone to decide. However, people who wish to buy expensive goods on credit often have their credit-worthiness examined before the retailer allows them to take the merchandise. This would tend to reduce this potential problem.

(e) *Housing*

Access to shops can affect individuals in terms of where they wish to live. Nearness to shopping facilities is often mentioned in estate agents' descriptions of houses. This can be of great important to old people and mothers with young children.

(t) *Staff*

(i) Transport problems — for those who work in the town centres and live in outlying areas, this also applies to other groups of workers. Additionally, the relatively high cost of transport poses problems.

(ii) Unsocial hours problem — Staff need to work Saturdays, six day trading is expected by customers, also late night shopping.

3.3 *Physical distribution*

(a) *Introduction*

Physical distribution is the name given to those activities which are concerned with the actual movement of goods from one place to another. You will see that Chapter 4 deals with the chain of distribution and mentions the channels used to distribute goods. The main components of physical distribution are transport and storage.

(b) *Transport*

The need to meet the huge demand for a vast range of products has lead to massive investment in and expansion of our transport system. The two main modes of transport used in distribution are:-

(i) *Rail*

Although since the 1960's the rail network has contracted, the introduction of liner trains, computer operated signals and improved rolling stock, have all contributed to the railways retention of much of their market.

(ii) *Road*

To move the quantities of goods required an extensive road network has developed including motorways which link manufacturers with wholesalers, retailers and customers.

This network carries many millions of tons of merchandise each day. The growing number of lorries which are necessary to carry these goods can have serious effects on the environment.

Vibration has caused serious damage to buildings. Fumes and noise have brought discomfort to many people. Commercial vehicles pay a high licence fee but some people argue this does not cover the damage done to roads and buildings.

The well developed transport system enables goods to be made available to the customer sometimes within a matter of hours or less of having been created e.g. bread. Fast specially equipped vehicles e.g. refrigerated lorries ensure that food can be delivered in a fresh condition. Many large scale retailers and manufacturers have their own fleets of delivery vehicles.

3.4   *Storage* (see also 12.3)

Many large and sophisticated warehouses and storage systems have been developed to meet the needs of distribution. Some, such as the North Eastern Co-op's warehouse in Peterlee are under computer control.

These facilities help manufacturers by enabling goods to be made and stored in advance of need e.g. toys for Christmas. This helps to ensure the continuity which is necessary to make modern mass production efficient and economical.

This storage facility is also useful to the retailer who has limited storage space. Wholesalers (see 4.4) who provide this and other services to many small scale retailers have possibly helped a number of their customers to remain in business.

3.5   *Exercise 1*

1. What social function may a cornershop perform which might help account for its continued existence?

2. How has retailing developed to make itself more convenient?

3. How may retailing encourage people to steal?

4. What effects can heavy goods vehicles have on the environment and on individuals?

5. How does the availability of storage facilities help both the manufacturer and the retailer?

3.6   *Effects on town centres*

(a) *Introduction*

The two factors which have largely shaped our town centres are distribution and the motor car. There has been a growing tendency in recent years to exclude the car from town centres. This has been done by the provision of ring roads, which enables through-traffic to by pass town centres and by restrictions on city centre parking.

(b) *Incidence of distribution outlets in town centres*

If you stand in the main street of your town you will notice that most, if not all, of the buildings house retail outlets distributing a variety of goods and services, e.g. clothes, shoes, holidays and electrical goods. This was not always the case. Houses and small scale industrial enterprises used to be found in or near the town centres. They have largely disappeared and the land and buildings have been acquired by distributors. The demand for sites in city centres is such that very high rents and rates can be charged for them. Retailers are willing to bear these costs because of the large number of potential customers. Other possible uses for these sites, residential or industrial, are discouraged because of these high costs.

Some of these city centre sites are more attractive than others i.e. those on the corners created by the inter-section of two main shopping streets. These are known as 'PRIME SITES' and are much sought after and can command a premium price, since they are limited in number and are likely to attract more custom.

(c) *Activity after the shops close*

Our town centres tend to be bustling hives of activity up until the late afternoon when those who are working in the town and the crowds of shoppers go home. The closure of the majority of the shops between 5 and 6 p.m. results in almost deserted city centres.

(d) *Dereliction*

The recognised shopping areas in a town sometimes change due to development. Those stores which attract fewer customers may deteriorate in appearance and may in extreme cases become derelict.

(e) *Uniformity of town centres*

It has been said that many of our town centres now look alike in layout with the same types of shops and the same style of buildings. A number of points can be advanced in support of this view.

(i) *The destruction of distinctive old buildings.*

Modern buildings tend to be less expensive to maintain and heat. A new store can be purpose built to minimise costs and maximise likely sales. Many town centres have been 'developed' by property companies and town councils. The developer acquires a number of valuable properties and the council benefits from increased rates.

(ii) *Traffic free shopping precincts*

These are areas from which motor traffic other than delivery vehicles, are excluded. This enables shoppers to move from one shop to another, safe from traffic dangers. More and more towns are introducing these traffic free shopping precincts.

(iii) *Growth of the multiples (see 5.4)*

These retailing organisations have expanded to the point where many have at least one branch in most large towns. These stores, as well as selling the same goods at the same prices in each town also have the same signs and colour schemes. A city centre street in a Northern town with a branch shop of each of Boots, C & A, Halfords, Marks and Spencers and British Homes Stores would appear very similar to one in a southern town in which the same organisations were represented.

(f) *Restrictions on cars*

City centre shops attract customers many of whom would like to park their cars as near as possible to the shops they use. This is not practicable. To limit the number of cars in shopping centres a number of measures have been taken:-

(i) Restrictions are placed on roadside parking — yellow lines and parking meters;

(ii) Out-of-town parking facilities often serviced by a regular bus shuttle service have been created;

(iii) Multi-storey car parks have been built, within a short walking distance of the main shopping area;

(iv) Traffic free shopping precincts have been made;
(see 3.5e)

(g) *Shopping centres*

These differ from the traffic free shopping precincts in that they are purpose built, the former consists largely of existing shopping facilities from which traffic has been excluded.

The first shopping centre was opened in Cowley, Oxfordshire as a suburban shopping centre. Several of the more recent ones are totally enclosed and have been situated more centrally.

The Eldon Square shopping centre in Newcastle-upon-Tyne built on two levels is totally enclosed. The hundred plus stores in the centre include major stores. Additionally pubs, recreational facilities e.g. judo and squash, and other facilities such as amenities for the disabled have also been provided.

A report by the Economic Development Council for the Distributive Trades published in 1968, on the Cowley Shopping Centre highlighted the following factors as being particularly important to the success of suburban shopping centres:-

(i) There is a need for a supermarket in such a centre — to enable potential customers to recoup additional travel costs;

(ii) The centres need to be sited in areas which have a sufficiently large pool of potential customers;

(iii) The need for good transport facilities particularly parking and bus services;

(iv) The need for publicity, especially in the early stages of development.

(h) *Out-of-town shopping*

The location of substantial shopping facilities outside town centres, either in the form of Shopping Centres or as Hypermarkets. (see 5.10) can have adverse effects on town centre shopping. The out-of-town facilities are developed to take advantage of the availability and lower costs of land (whether renting or buying) and lower rates.

Town centre shop owners usually object fiercely to any proposed development of such facilities. They argue that they have to pay high city centre costs and so are at a competitive disadvantage compared to out-of-town shopping centres.

3.7 *Exercise 2*

1. What is a 'Prime Site'. Give two local examples.

2. Many cities are very similar. What arguments can be put forward to support this view?

3. Give two examples of retailers and manufacturers who have their own delivery vehicles.

4. Explain in your own words the meaning of the term 'shopping centre'. Give a local example

5. Why have out-of-town shopping facilities?

3.8 **Assignments**

1. Draw up a plan of the main shopping street giving the occupier of each building. State which of those may be found in other towns' main shopping streets.

2. From you own research such as talking to older relatives, list the major changes in your or a neighbouring town in the last twenty years.

Chapter 4

Chain of Distribution

At the end of this Chapter you should be able to:-

(A) Draw and describe the chain of distribution.

(B) List the functions of a wholesaler.

(C) Identify and give examples of the different types of wholesalers with particular reference to their operation and how they satisfy the demands of their customers.

(D) Compare the arguments for and against wholesalers.

(E) Describe direct selling methods.

(F) Explain the purpose of Marketing Boards.

(G) Describe co-operative marketing organisations.

4.1   Raw materials are extracted and manufactured to produce consumer goods which satisfy our needs. These goods then pass through the wholesaler to the retailer and finally reach the consumer. At each stage value is added to the goods, i.e. they become worth more money as they pass through the stages of transformation. An example of this would be to follow the production of a table from the tree, through the manufacturer, to the retailer. It is easy to see that finished tables are worth more than the tree, standing in a forest, from which they are made. The tables now have a specific use and can satisfy the needs of a customer whereas the tree is unable to do this whilst it is still growing. See Exhibit 4.01.

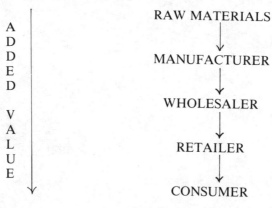

Exhibit 4.01
The Chain of Distribution

This system also applies to food; take peas for instance. These are grown by the farmer who sells them to a manufacturer e.g. canner or freezer, who then distributes them to the retailer. Regardless of where the raw materials originate, they must pass through all these stages. We return to this aspect in paragraph 4.9 when discussing goods which appear to by-pass the chain.

One thing common to all the stages of production is transport. Without transport the goods could not be transferred between each stage. Only in a few cases do raw materials become ready for the consumer without being moved from one organisation to another. During the last few years there have been many examples of shortages due to breakdowns in the transport system, e.g. strikes of tanker drivers and bread delivery men.

We will now deal with each stage in turn and examine its functions and importance.

4.2 *Manufacturer*

Manufacturers process raw materials and turn them into marketable merchandise. They buy from either local or foreign producers, usually on a contract basis e.g. the large freezing companies will arrange with a farmer to purchase a whole field of peas which are harvested when ready. This is an example of large scale production run by companies or groups of companies. At the other end are single units or people working on their own to produce goods or provide services which satisfy consumer needs e.g. an artist or a wood carver.

Manufacturers can either produce a wide range of lines or concentrate on one only. They may diversify and produce a very wide range of seemingly unrelated items e.g. soap, margarine, fats, perfume or tinned food. They offer a delivery service and they have representatives who promote sales.

Another useful service provided by manufacturers is that of advertising their products. This 'brings them' before the public. It maintains the production of standard lines and helps to promote new lines. See 16.1d.

4.3 *Wholesaler*

The wholesaler takes the goods produced by the manufacturer and distributes them to the retailer. This system developed after medieval times when there was very little wholesaling done (see 1.6). It was after this period that wholesalers became established and improved the means of distribution. They would buy in advance from the producer, using their skills to anticipate demand and then transport the goods to the retailer.

4.4 *Functions of a wholesaler*
(a) They buy in advance, anticipating the demands of the retailer. Years of experience have taught them which are the best selling lines. Their skill is used to advantage, especially when buying seasonal goods, e.g. Easter eggs or Christmas stock. These items are usually ordered some six to eight months before the event. The wholesaler takes delivery and pays for them at least three months before the retailer decides to buy.

All the risk in buying is taken by the wholesaler who stands to lose a considerable amount of money when wrong decisions are made. The profit margin is quite small on most items. Losses would therefore take a long time to recoup.

(b) The warehousing function is essential in providing a steady market in which manufacturers can operate. Wholesalers buy in bulk from manufacturers, thus allowing space in the factory for the manufacturers to continue producing. The manufacturer is also paid for the goods, which in turn allows him to make further purchases of raw materials. Wholesalers also provide storage for retailers allowing them to buy in small quantities. Thus the retailer will not have to 'tie up' large sums in stock — all of which have to be paid for. Retailers require a wide range of goods from which to choose in order to satisfy the needs of their customers. Neither the manufacturer nor the retailer are equipped to hold large stocks of merchandise.

(c) It is easy to see from (b), that indirectly the wholesaler provides finance for both the manufacturer and the retailer. From the manufacturer the wholesaler buys merchandise in bulk and pays for it quickly. The wholesaler helps the retailer financially by storing goods for him to purchase in small quantities.

(d) All traditional wholesalers provide delivery services, representatives who promote and sell goods, and credit. See 4.7a

(e) The wholesaler provides a link between the manufacturer and the retailer by passing on information about market trends, prices, ideas and criticisms.

4.5   Necessity of the wholesaler

It has been said by many that a wholesaler is an unnecessary link in the chain of distribution. Some people argue that the wholesaler creates an increase in the price of goods which does nothing to improve their value.

If the wholesaler were eliminated, the functions in 4.4 would have to be performed by the manufacturer and/or the retailer. Consider the plight of a manufacturer who prefers to deal direct with the retailer. Storage areas would have to be built, delivery services provided, and a back-up administration centre to deal with enquiries, invoices and payments. With manufacturers enforcing minimum quantities for delivery, the very small retailer would not be contacted. In turn this would reduce the number of outlets selling those products.

Many multiples and supermarkets perform this function themselves so that the wholesaling function does not disappear in these circumstances.

Wholesalers are necessary because they:-

(a) give more efficient distribution;

(b) contact small retailers thus improving the distribution of merchandise;

(c) lower the costs for both manufacturer and retailer by storing goods in anticipation of demand which in turn releases capital 'tied up' in stock. See 4.4b;

(d) provide a distribution service for the small manufacturer;

(e) anticipate seasonal demands.

4.6 *Exercise 1*

1. List the links in the chain of distribution.
2. Explain why transport is important to distribution.
3. Briefly describe the functions of a manufacturer.
4. List the functions of a wholesaler.
5. Why are wholesalers necessary?

4.7 *Types of wholesaler*

(a) *Traditional wholesaler*

These provide a very wide range of goods under one roof, in a warehouse divided into specialised departments. They also provide a delivery service, credit, and representatives. In most cases the retailer does not visit the warehouse, but transacts business through the representative who used to be known as 'Commercial travellers'. For seasonal trade, e.g. choosing summer fashions, the wholesaler may invite retailers to browse around a showroom before placing an order.

(b) *Specialist wholesalers*

These provide a similar service to the traditional wholesaler but operate on a much smaller scale. They usually specialise in a narrow range of related products e.g. continental foods.

(c) *Cash and carry wholesalers*

These function as their title implies. The retailer pays cash for the goods and carries them away. He will choose goods from the warehouse, put them on a trolley and take them to a checkout area for payment. After payment the goods are loaded into the retailer's transport and taken back to the shop. This eliminates all the traditional functions of a wholesaler such as delivery, representatives, credit and bad debts. As a result, prices can be reduced, examples of cash and carry wholesalers are Makro and Alliance.

Retailers can buy any quantity and if a cash and carry wholesaler has not got any items the retailer can then try elsewhere. He will know immediately whether or not the wholesaler is out of stock. He may well have placed orders with traditional wholesalers, and found that there are many times when items are 'crossed off' the delivery and where it is often too late to try another firm. In most cases cash and carry wholesalers have late night opening for retailers who are unable to come during the day.

One problem associated with 'cash and carries' is that of providing goods to bona fide retailers. A minimum of one item can be bought for example, electrical goods. Some members of the general public are using, or are trying to use, the services of this type of wholesaler.

Strict controls must be operated by the use of identity cards, proof of business interest, and signing-in procedures.

(d) *Voluntary groups and chains*

These were started to help small retailers meet competition from large retailing outlets. A group consists of either:-

(i) a wholesaler and a number of retailers who have agreed to buy all their goods from him.

(ii) a group of retailers who have combined to perform their own wholesaling function and to deal with numerous manufacturers.

A chain is a combination of wholesalers spread throughout the country who supply a large number of retailers. These are usually called 'Symbol' groups e.g. SPAR.

Symbol groups help the independent retailer to maintain a share of the market in the face of competition. They offer:-

(i)   discount prices;

(ii)   special offers;

(iii) a first class wholesaling service with a wide range of goods;

(iv)   good delivery service to reduce 'out of stock' positions;

(v)   proprietary or own brand labels;

(vi)   back up service such as store layouts and advice;

(vii) computerised invoice systems for accurate margin control;

(viii) local support service such as advertising and special promotions.

For this system to be efficient the retailer must:-

(i)   buy all his goods from the group wholesaler;

(ii)   participate in group promotions;

(iii) be of a certain size and buying power;

(iv)   own a shop which is up to standard or can be altered to meet the requirements;

(v)   display the group symbol.

4.8 One of the main problems when dealing with a wholesaler is that of 'crossed off' items on delivery. To eliminate this the retailer could use the services of a cash and carry wholesaler in order to avoid and 'out of stock' position. See 4.7c

In general, wholesalers can be grouped as:-

(a) National, which consists of very large general or specialised wholesalers;

(b) Regional, who meet the needs of retailers in a particular area;

(c) Local, who provide a service for a town or city.

Many national wholesalers are springing up near the networks of good trunk roads or within easy motorway access in order to draw from a larger area.

4.9 Alternatives to the wholesaler

There are other alternatives which bypass the wholesaler and are classed as direct selling.

(a) *Direct selling between producer and consumer.*

A good example is the farmer or florist selling produce at the gate. These are found on country roads and are inexpensive to run. They do not require staff to stand behind the table, but utilise employees working in the fields or garden. By this method the producer can earn a little extra profit with very little outlay. A further example is the farmer with a stall in an open air retail market.

Direct selling

(b) *Direct selling between manufacturers and consumers.*

Here manufacturers set up their own retail outlets e.g. Brentford Nylons. Only when production is on a large scale can manufacturers operate their own retail shops. Further examples are mail order, direct representation or door-to-door selling. Products sold by this method include office equipment, brushes and cosmetics.

(c) *Direct selling between manufacturer and retailer.*

Here manufacturers service retail outlets from the stock they produce. Take for example the direct selling of tights or stockings. The retailers stands or shelves are filled by van salesmen at regular intervals. The retailer only pays for the goods he has purchased for filling up the stands. Sales by this method have become more common as the scale of production has increased. Another example would be a farmer selling in a wholesale market.

In general, provided production can be maintained at a high level, manufacturers prefer to employ their own salesmen who sell direct to the retailer and run their own distribution system. Salesmen will thus concentrate only on the products of one manufacturer, whereas a wholesaler will sell many similar lines which can be readily interchanged.

4.10 *Marketing boards*

These were set up to regulate the marketing of some types of agricultural produce e.g. milk. The Milk Marketing Board set up by the Government controls the payments for milk, and maintains a fixed price in a region. All the milk is pooled and distributed from a central dairy. This standardises any slight fluctuations in quality from farmer to farmer. The Boards also act as an intermediary between producer and retailer by providing dairy facilities; or producer and consumer with advertising and promotions.

4.11 *Co-operative marketing organisations*

These were established to market produce e.g. fruit and vegetables from individual growers. They collect, select, grade, and pack the produce. It is then sold to the wholesaler or central market e.g. Covent Garden. This co-ordinates the activities of many small growers who receive a better price for their produce than they would if they marketed it on their own. See also 5.8 which deals with the Co-operative movement.

4.12 *Exercise 2*

1. Describe the functions of a traditional wholesaler.
2. Why are cash and carry wholesalers beneficial to the small retailer?
3. List the benefits to the small retailer offered by 'Symbol' groups.
4. What are voluntary groups and chains?
5. List the alternative methods of selling which bypass the wholesaler. Give examples.
6. Describe a co-operative marketing association.

4.13 **Assignments**

1. Select a product you handle and are familiar with. Progress it through the chain of distribution starting with it in the raw state. Briefly describe the various stages through which it passes.
2. Investigate the different methods your store uses when purchasing goods for re-sale. List and describe the reasons for using each method. You will require the assistance of your manager or the owner of the business.

Chapter 5

Types of Shops

At the end of this chapter you should be able to:-

(A) Explain the need for enterprise.

(B) List the advantages and disadvantages of sole proprietors, partnerships and companies.

(C) Identify and give examples of the types of retail organisations.

(D) Describe their historical development.

(E) Describe their operation.

(F) Identify their characteristics.

(G) Draw organisation charts for each type.

(H) Explain the ways in which each satisfies the needs of their customers.

(J) Interpret statistical information on their own growth and decline.

5.1 As we have already seen, the retailer completes the chain of distribution by finally bringing the goods to the consumer. He allows them choice by satisfying their needs. In 3.5 we looked at the problems faced by retailers due to the changing face of inner city areas and the emergence of precincts and traffic free shopping. There must be a wide variety of shops in order to maintain a balanced shopping area which will attract a broad section of the community. In addition there must be facilities for parking plus accessible public transport.

In any town or city there are many types of shops available to meet the needs of the general public. They will include some or all of the following list:-

(a) Unit shops e.g. market or street trader, corner shop;

(b) Multiples e.g. Burtons, John Collier, Richard Shops;

(c) Variety chains e.g. Woolworths, Littlewoods, Marks & Spencers;

(d) Department Stores e.g. Selfridges, Debenhams, Harrods;

(e) Co-operatives;

(f) Supermarkets e.g. Tesco, Sainsburys;

(g) Hypermarkets e.g. Carrefour, Co-op.

We will look at the historical development and organisation of each of these types of retail outlet.

5.2 *Enterprise*

There is need for growth in business in order to expand and to meet constant change. The basic ingredient of growth is capital, i.e. money used in a business to buy for example land, buildings, equipment or stock. Capital can come from many sources. In the case of the sole trader it can take the form of his own savings or other people's savings e.g. bank loan or even a windfall such as a win on the football pools. If money is limited, or hard to acquire by these methods, he may invite someone to join him in business. This person would put an agreed amount of money into the business and become a partner. They would then share both the work and any profit or losses made by the venture. This is the first occasion on which losses have been mentioned. In the case of a sole trader or partnership, both could lose a considerable amount of money and possessions in the event of a business becoming bankrupt. When this happens most of the private possessions of the sole trader or partner can be taken from them, and sold to provide cash to settle the debts of the business.

One of the ways to guard one's personal possessions against possible action such as this is to form a limited liability company. Here no member can be asked to pay more into the company than the cost of the shares bought. This safeguards personal savings and possessions if the company gets into a position where it cannot meet its debts.

This allows for further expansion where people can invite their friends and relatives to join by forming a private limited company. If such a venture becomes highly successful they may convert the private limited company into a public limited company. Anyone may then buy shares and such an inflow of cash will allow for further expansion.

There are certain legal limitations when forming companies. In addition the Stock Exchange would have to approve and control any dealings in public limited company shares. Each type of organisation has its own advantages and disadvantages. See Exhibit 5.01.

Another form of enterprise has been developed by co-operation. There are both productive, wholesale and retail co-operative systems. See 4.11 and 5.8 for a full explanation of their growth and organisation.

Enterprise is not limited to private individuals investing their personal savings. The Government controls a large number of retail outlets through its nationalised industries, e.g. Electricity and Gas Showrooms and the Post Office. These are public corporations financed by every tax paying person in the U.K. They have a vast turnover and employ thousands of people whose job it is to sell direct to the general public.

Here we see that an enterprise can be in the hands of one person or many people. Business involves many risks (e.g. will people buy what I am offering for sale?). Without risk takers who are often the people advancing the capital, there would be no business.

Every organisation has its own particular way of satisfying the needs of its customers and would include some or all of the following methods:-

(a) Personal service;
(b) Self service;
(c) Price — price reductions or special offers;
(d) Variety — wide range of goods to choose from;
(e) Surroundings — clean, bright, clear aisles;
(f) Supporting services — delivery, credit, after-sales service.

ADVANTAGES	DISADVANTAGES
Sole Proprietor	
Independence	Unlimited liability
Personal contact	Difficult to expand
Close control	Lack of versatility
Flexibility	Initial capital small
Freedom of action	Working capital small
Simple organisation	Bears all the worry
Partnerships	
More capital than sole trader	Unlimited liability
Personal contact	Can create disagreements
Can involve specialist partners	Not easy to dissolve
Easier expansion	Can have long discussions
Shared strain	Shared profits
Shared losses	Membership not transferrable
Limited Companies	
Limited liability	Often lack of personal contact
Ability to raise capital	High formation expenses
Membership can be transferred	Covered by regulations
Continuity	Slow decisions
Larger buying units (better terms)	

Exhibit 5.01
Types of Business Organization

5.3 *Unit shops*

These are mainly run by sole traders, i.e. private or independent retailers. They sell a wide variety of goods and usually depend on personal contact backed by supporting services such as late openings, convenience, satisfaction of local needs.

A sole trader is a person who prefers to trade on his own and not join a partnership or company. Aptly described as a "lone wolf", he is free to take any decision he feels is right.

Many establishments are 'passed down' through families and have been in the same hands for generations. Some set up in business because they wish to work for themselves, often having had experience in other working environments. The amount of hard work done by a sole trader — the long hours and total dedication to the job for relatively little return — are often not appreciated. There is now an enormous amount of paperwork which is often done in spare time or at weekends, e.g. wages, VAT, accounts.

These retailers use the services of the cash and carry wholesaler or are affiliated to voluntary groups or chains as outlined in 4.7c and 4.7d.

All the organising is done by the owner who may run the business either by himself or with his wife, or by employing one or two assistants on a full or part time basis. Many of these units expand by buying other shops, which in turn increases the amount of work for the owner. He would then expand the enterprise as previously described.

5.4 Multiples

The definition of a multiple shop is one which is operated by a retail business having ten or more branches. Ownership started in the hands of only a few enterprising people. Today's multiples are public limited companies with a turnover of millions of pounds. In the early days it was the onset of cheaper food and mass produced goods on which a company thrived. Their surroundings were considered rather spartan by comparison to the more elaborate emporiums. Only a limited range of reasonably priced fast selling products were sold. This is still true of today's multiples. The present trend is towards larger units which take advantage of bulk buying, larger discounts and competitive prices. These advantages lead to a large turnover with relatively low operating costs.

They often deal in only one commodity group such as ladies or men's fashions and shoes. Layout and systems are standardised throughout the branches giving a readily recognisable image e.g. shop fronts, uniforms, window displays, price tickets and advertising.

Most multiples have their own warehousing operation referred to in 4.5 where goods are bought centrally and distributed to regional depots which, in turn, distribute to shops in the area. They need to be sited in a busy street with plenty of passing trade. See 3.5 where the location of stores was discussed.

5.5 Exercise 1

1. List the types of shops usually found in towns and cities.
2. In what ways can a sole proprietor expand his business.

3. Name three advantages and disadvantages of —
   (a) sole proprietor
   (b) partnership
   (c) company
4. Explain the organisation of a unit shop.
5. Define a multiple and give an example.
6. How do multiples satisfy the needs of their customers.

5.6 Variety chains

Variety chains are by definition multiples but differ from them as they deal in a variety of goods and do not specialise in one particular grouping. Imagine you are standing in the centre of your local Woolworths — the range of goods you will see is enormous.

Many have their own brand name, e.g. Marks & Spencer is 'St. Michael', which helps to promote their image and keep it before the public.

All variety chains have turned over to self selection from open displays of clearly priced goods. They also take advantage of bulk buying, larger discounts, and competitive prices. These advantages lead to a large turnover with relatively low operating costs.

5.7 Department stores

These can be described as shops within a shop. Here there is a large retail shop with various floors or departments dealing in separate goods. They provide a complete range of services under one roof.

The ownership of these varies from store to store as some are large nationally known companies e.g. Selfridges — to small local companies owned by a family.

Emphasis is on service which involves a high degree of expense. This would include delivery, credit, accounts, restaurants, hair dressing salons, carpeted floors, lifts and personal service. Many lease areas for other retailers to sell their own goods, especially through demonstrations. Those who are members of large groups take advantage of bulk buying and the sharing of administration costs.

5.8 Co-operatives See also 4.11

Co-operation is a means of self help in business where a few people join together and establish their own organisation.

The Co-operative movement was started in 1844 by the 28 Rochdale Pioneers. Each subscribed £1 to the venture. With this money they bought food in bulk and sold it back to themselves at the full retail price. Any profit made at the end of a trading period was divided between them in proportion to the amount of goods bought.

Co-operatives differ from other outlets because they are owned and controlled by many of the people who shop there.

Membership is open to all who subscribe to a share and each member can participate in the running of the Society by voting at meetings. Their votes elect the Board of Directors who are responsible for policy decisions. There are still some small independent Co-ops run by this method who issue a dividend. In recent years many have either gone out of business or joined the Co-operative Retail Services Ltd. This is a national organisation established by the Co-operative Wholesale Society Ltd., and was set up to take over retail societies which were in danger of closing down due to lack of customers or falling profits. They consolidated the trading in large areas by closing many of the small uneconomic shops and transferring business to larger more efficient branches. One of the early ideas of the Co-operative movement was to have a large number of shops conveniently placed in high population areas. Another function of C.R.S. Ltd. was to look at areas which had no co-operative services with a view to setting up businesses there.

There are many advantages in this form of co-operation. Customers hold shares which in turn breeds customer loyalty. They can associate themselves with the running of the Society which stimulates their desire to buy goods from it. All the benefits of bulk buying are passed on to the customer in the form of cut prices. The majority of societies give instant dividend in the form of trading stamps, see also 16.8a. On the other hand there are some disadvantages. They have been very slow to develop their image, possibly due to the fact that the Committees elected to control policies had very little business experience. New ideas were never forthcoming which accounted for the Co-op's stereotyped, staid outlook. Small societies are inefficient and unable to compete with larger ones. Some people may object to the Co-ops having their own political party.

5.9 *Supermarkets*

Supermarkets started in America where they originally consisted of many different traders all under one roof. The owners of the market would rent areas to traders, similar to today's covered markets run by Local Authorities. Prior to 1930 they consisted of very large markets, an example of which was the Piggly Wiggly Stores. In 1916 Clarence Saunders started this first self service store in Memphis Tennessee, and later it developed into a large chain.

Between 1930 and 1935 came the 'cheapy' markets e.g. King Kullen Market opened in 1930 on Long Island, New York, with low priced goods in very spartan surroundings. These would be similar to some of today's discount stores opened in rented property with poor quality fixtures and bare walls.

From 1935 onwards the 'cheapies' lost favour and supermarkets began to develop until they reached their present day form. The Royal Arsenal Co-op produced the first supermarket in this country during 1948. Supermarkets developed due to a shortage of staff during a period of high employment. Their operation has been improved due to the abolition of price maintenance and the introduction of large negotiable discounts for bulk buying.

A supermarket is a self service store of more than 4000 sq. ft. of selling area and more than three checkouts. Those below this size are classed as mini-markets. Supermarkets have created many advantages from the owners point of view — they require less staff for a high volume of sales. In addition more stock is on show and cash sales eliminate bad debts. The customers benefit from reduced prices, special offers, quick comparison of products and a wide range of goods under one roof. Customers can shop at their own speed and in their own time e.g. late night openings. One big advantage is the growth of large car parks for the convenience of the motoring public.

There are however, certain disadvantages such as the reduction in personal service and lack of supporting services e.g. delivery. Time can be wasted in looking for goods and in waiting at the checkouts, especially at crowded peak shopping periods. There is a tendency for customers to buy on impulse which creates embarrassment at the checkouts due to overspending. Sites are not always conveniently placed except for the motorist, which creates difficulties for children and the elderly. It is not always possible to send a child into a supermarket to do the shopping. One major disadvantage which has grown with supermarketing and open displays is that of stealing — see 10.5f and 13.4.

5.10 Hypermarkets

These can be described as super-supermarkets with a selling area of at least 25,000 sq. ft. operating by self service with more than 15 checkouts. The first opened in France during 1963 at St. Genevieve des Bois. In the U.K. the first was opened during 1972 at Caerphilly in South Wales. Both ventures attracted a great deal of argument, much of it coming from town centre traders who feared their turnover would drop considerably. The preservationists were concerned with the loss of more Green Belt land and objected strongly at public enquiries and planning permission meetings.

Hypermarkets are usually situated at the edge of towns and cities away from the centre, with very large parking areas. An ideal position would be alongside a network of major ring roads or motorways bringing customers from a wide area.

5.11 Gas and Electricity Showrooms

These sell appliances in addition to providing an installation and repair service. Electricity Boards have to compete with other large retailing outlets e.g. discount stores and multiples. They all sell electrical appliances which only require plugging in to a source of supply. On the other hand there is little competition for the Gas Boards as gas installations require specialist knowledge and cannot be done by amateurs. Both Boards act as a collecting point for the payment of accounts in addition to giving information and advice.

—Retail and Service Trade Summaries by form of organisation and broad kind of business, 1961, 1966, 1971

Kind of business	Establishments			Turnover			Persons engaged		
	1961	1966	1971	1961	1966	1971	1961	1966	1971
	Number	Number	Number	£'000	£'000	£'000	Number	Number	Number
TOTAL RETAIL TRADE	..	..	..	9,253,779	11,757,314	16,685,462	..	..	..
Retail shops	542,301	504,412	472,991	8,828,111	11,131,816	15,610,730	2,484,622	2,555,737	2,541,430
Co-operative societies	29,396	26,684	15,413	959,339	1,015,938	1,107,999	195,144	173,458	132,204
Multiples	66,701	73,852	66,785	2,578,898	3,837,244	6,083,560	632,661	741,833	814,666
Independents	446,204	403,876	390,793	5,289,875	6,278,634	8,419,171	1,656,817	1,640,446	1,594,560
Grocers and provision dealers	146,777	123,385	105,283	2,350,711	2,907,655	4,156,487	551,601	522,343	542,676
Other food retailers	114,655	104,359	92,524	1,727,896	2,081,314	2,614,683	471,533	459,358	418,437
Confectioners, tobacconists, newsagents	70,108	63,333	52,064	797,832	1,045,572	1,305,875	249,853	297,762	275,458
Clothing and footwear shops	86,555	83,095	81,279	1,366,737	1,719,336	2,371,766	396,996	410,503	403,744
Household goods shops	60,343	65,850	70,342	948,335	1,292,186	2,006,634	264,686	289,549	289,691
Other non-food retailers	60,113	61,381	66,724	706,913	1,019,225	1,568,726	237,208	269,738	298,043
General stores	3,750	3,009	4,775	929,687	1,066,529	1,586,559	312,745	306,484	313,381
Market stalls and mobile shops	35,006	..	31,790	90,749	..	146,965	39,462	..	37,829
Electricity and Gas Board showrooms	2,791	3,012	2,359	104,174	185,780	283,300	..	..	10,579
Mail order businesses	556	495	771	226,673	428,834	632,585	40,589	54,787	59,816
Automatic vending machine operators	26	56	65	4,072	10,884	11,882	992	2,156	1,787
SERVICE TRADES									
Footwear repairing establishments	11,154	8,769	5,494	25,436	26,039	22,412	24,183	19,154	10,996
Hairdressing establishments	40,152	47,632	47,191	97,267	135,823	166,158	139,175	163,298	154,950
Laundries, laundrette operators and dry cleaners	4,573	5,621	8,405	112,483	172,287	212,349	136,819	141,329	115,488
TOTAL RETAIL TRADE AND SERVICE TRADES	..	..	..	9,488,966	12,091,463	17,086,381	..	..	..

Exhibit 5.02

5.12 *Industrial Selling* — See Chapter 7

5.13 *Exercise 2*

1. Describe a variety chain and give an example.
2. How do department stores satisfy the needs of their customers?
3. Describe a retail co-operative and explain how they started.
4. In what ways do co-operatives differ from other retail organisations?
5. Briefly describe the historical development of supermarkets.
6. Define a supermarket and explain how they meet the needs of their customers.
7. Define a hypermarket.
8. What arguments are made against the building of hypermarkets?

5.14 **Assignments**

1. Investigate the shop in which you are employed. Briefly explain its history including:-

   (a) who started it,

   (b) where it started,

   (c) why it started,

   (d) what changes have been made since starting,

   (e) outline the types of goods sold over the period.

   State how it satisfies the needs of customers, looking at product range, price, services, opening hours or any other relevant facilities.

2. Take a specific area in a busy part of your own town or city. It could be a precinct, street or shopping complex. List the shops in the area noting the types of goods sold. Divide these into categories as defined in the chapter. How do these shops meet the needs of their customers.

Chapter 6

Selling Without Shops

At the end of this chapter you should be able to:-
(A) List the various non-shop methods of distribution.
(B) Give appropriate examples of them.
(C) Explain briefly how each one operates.
(D) Explain the reasons for their growth.

6.1   *Reasons for not selling through shops.*

No doubt you recall from the first chapter that it is not necessary to have a shop in order to distribute goods. Various other methods have been found, in some ways better suited to distribute certain goods than the more usual shop.

Benefits which can accrue from not using retail shops can include

(a)   Reduction in the costs of operation, e.g. shop rents, rates and staff wages;

(b)   More flexibility because not 'tied' to shop opening hours which are limited by law.

6.2   *Door-to-door selling*

This occurs when the person who is doing the selling calls at the door of potential customer and either demonstrates the product(s) or tries to make a sale on the door step:-

(a)   Milk and dairy products by milk roundsmen;

(b)   Clothes pegs and 'lucky' charms often by gypsies;

(c)   Brushes were at one time sold in this manner, although like the travelling tinker this method seems to have virtually disappeared;

Door-to-door selling is also used to sell more expensive items such as sets of encyclopaedias, insurance, double glazing, and expensive items of household equipment, e.g. vacuum cleaners.

Sometimes the salesman calls as a result of a request from a potential customer. More often the sales person just calls without any prior intimation that the customer is interested in the products for sale. This is known as "cold canvassing" and usually has a poor ratio of sales to calls.

The main advantage is one of convenience especially for those who cannot always get to the shops, e.g. elderly people, invalids and those with very young children. It is also useful as a delivery service for goods in regular demand.

Door-to-door selling tends not to have a very good reputation, many of those who sell by this method are paid wholly or in part on a commission basis. This may mean a temptation to use high pressure sales techniques to sell goods people don't really want in order to earn more money.

Public disquiet over this method of selling has resulted in government legislation to protect the consumer. First, the Consumer Credit Act of

But we've already got one

1974 ensures that if the customer signs a credit agreement at home (for more than £30) she has time to think about it and if she so wishes can then cancel the agreement. This must be done in writing within five days of the customer receiving a second copy of the agreement through the post.

Secondly, the Office of Fair Trading publishes a very useful leaflet entitled "How To Cope With Door Step Salesmen." It describes various ploys used by salesmen in order to gain entrance/make sales and offers advice on how to deal with the situation.

6.3 *Automatic vending*

This method of distributing goods has enjoyed a high degree of growth in the last twenty years or so although it has been in existence for over a century. See exhibit 6.01.

Table 26—Automatic Vending Machine Operators: Commodity Sales, 1961, 1966, 1971

Commodity sold	1961	1966	1971
	£'000	£'000	£'000
TOTAL	**4,072**	**10,884**	**11,882**
Cigarettets and tobacco	1,427	5,767	4,779
Chocolate and sugar confectionary	1,861	2,047	797
Milk	252	214	39
Other cold drinks	⎤	296	844
Hot drinks	⎟	1,714	4,008
Food and snacks	532	292	479
Other sales	⎦	212	449
Subsidies from firms for operating machines on their premises		342	485

Exhibit 6.01
Source: Census of Distribution

Appropriate coins are fed into the machine. One follows the simple instructions and (in most cases!) the goods are delivered to you.

Numerous comparatively inexpensive and small items are sold in this way e.g. cigarettes, chocolate, hot and cold drinks and snacks. The advantages of this form of distribution are:-

(a) The service operates for 24 hours a day, although the place where they are situated may close, e.g. some late night petrol stations;

(b) It requires little attention other than re-stocking, removing cash and occasional servicing;

The disadvantages are:-

(a) Sometimes they fail to operate;

(b) They are prone to vandalism and robbery if not located in a safe place.

6.4 Party selling

This is a comparatively novel method of distributing certain types of merchandise to women, most of whom are housewives. It has been used to sell amongst other items — household plastic containers, jewellery, cosmetics and clothes.

Someone organises a 'party' at their house, this may be nothing more elaborate than the serving of tea or coffee and light refreshments to invited friends, neighbours and relatives. In the course of the evening the products for sale are shown and the participants invited to make purchases.

The 'Party Giver' receives payment either in cash or goods on the basis of what has been sold.

The advantages to the customer are the enjoyment of the social gathering and the opportunity to see and try the merchandise in relaxed surroundings.

The advantages to the distributor of party selling are that the costs are minimal and that most people buy something.

6.5 Exercises 1

1. What advantages are there in distributing goods other than through a shop?

2. What steps have been taken to protect consumers from unscrupulous Door-To-Door Salesmen?

3. As a salesman selling vending machines what selling points would you put to a potential customer?

4. Why is the 'Party' method of selling so called?

5. List four items which may be distributed in this way.

6.6 Mail Order (1) Catalogues

This method of distributing goods is widely used, mainly by housewives. See exhibit 6.02

Table 20—Mail order sales by form of organisation and kind of business, 1961, 1966, 1971

Form of organisation and kind of business	1961	1966	1971
	£ million	£ million	£ million
Total Mail Order Sales by Retail Organisations	**238.6**	**441.6**	**652.0**
Total sales of mail order businesses	226.7	428.8	632.6
General mail order houses	205.4	383.7	537.2
Other mail order businesses	21.3	45.2	95.4
Mail order sales of multiple retailers with 10 or more establishments	1.5	4.3	6.5
Department stores	0.0	0.0	*
Other kinds of business	1.5	4.3	*
Mail order sales of large independents	10.5	8.5	12.9
Department stores	3.5	4.3	4.1
Other kinds of business	7.0	4.2	8.8

Exhibit 6.02
Source: Census of Distribution

Several large organisations e.g. Great Universal Stores and Littlewoods have extensive mail order interests. Many of the catalogues produced by these and other firms are widely known i.e. Marshall Ward, John England and Janet Frazer.

An agent often a housewife, receives a large, maybe over 1,000 pages, lavishly illustrated book showing a range of merchandise comparable in scope with that seen in many department stores. This catalogue is shown to friends, neighbours and relatives who choose merchandise and pay the agent by instalments over a number of weeks.

The advantages of this method of distribution have resulted in its rapid and sustained growth — These are as follows:

(a) *For the customer:*

   (i) The convenience of armchair shopping — goods can be chosen at leisure in the home without long and possibly tedious shopping expeditions. Additionally there is no pressure to make a purchasing decision;

   (ii) Goods can be paid for by twenty weekly instalments or longer for more expensive goods;

   (iii) Goods on approval — if on examining goods at home the customer feels that for some reason they are unsuitable then they can be returned;

   (iv) There are no additional cost to customers e.g. postage, the goods are delivered to the home either direct or by the agent who also collects payments and credit is provided at no extra cost.

   (v) There is a wide range of good quality merchandise provided including branded goods;

40

40

(b) *For the agent:*

(i) The agent receives commission on the money remitted to the mail order company. This is usually 10% — 12½%. A slightly higher rate may be offered if goods rather than cash are accepted;

(ii) It provides an opportunity to meet regularly friends, neighbours and relatives.

(c) *For the Mail Order company*

(i) The costs of maintaining a large network of stores are avoided;

(ii) There is a large number of potential customers;

(iii) A certain amount of credit control and administrative paperwork is performed by the agents;

(iv) Warehousing and storage can be arranged so as to minimise rates and V.A.T.

The disadvantages of mail order selling are that:

(i) The goods tend to be relatively more expensive than in certain stores;

(ii) Interruptions in the postal service can obviously have, if only for a time, a serious effect on sales.

6.7 *Mail Order (2) Newspapers and magazines*

Many business offer their goods and services in newspapers, magazines and other publications. A glance at a number of these will show the wide range of these goods and services, e.g. greenhouses, household items, some clothing and cures for smoking.

Often businesses will offer their goods or services by advertising in a publication read by potential customers, e.g greenhouses will be advertised in gardening magazines or in the gardening part of the newspapers.

Goods and services sold in this manner tend not to be high value items, most people like to examine the more expensive items before buying.

Sometimes goods are offered as being direct from the manufacturer. Here the supplier 'cuts out' the retailer and the goods are said to be cheaper. However, this may not necessarily be the case. Since other costs have to be borne, i.e. advertising, postage and packing (often charged to the customer). There exists a number of safeguards to protect people who buy goods in this way.

(a) *Trade Descriptions Act 1968* – Very briefly and simply this law makes it a criminal offence for a trader falsely to describe goods or services. See exhibit 6.03.

(b) *Business Disclosure (Advertising) Act 1977* – requires advertisers to inform the public when advertising in classified columns if they are traders. See exhibit 6.04.

```
NOTICE TO
ADVERTISERS

TRADE DESCRIPTIONS ACT
1968

Advertisements will only be
accepted on the understanding
that descriptions relating to goods
are accurate and in no way
contravene the provisions of the
Trade Descriptions Act 1968.
```

Exhibit 6.03
An example of a notice found in newspapers

```
Important Notice to advertisers and
readers.
Business Disclosures (Advertising) Act, 1977
Our Post Classified columns contain advertisements from
private individuals and from traders.
It is the legal responsibility of the latter to make clear in
their advertisements that they
are in fact
TRADERS, DEALERS, MANUFACTURERS, AGENTS, Etc.
We will not knowingly accept trade advertisements which
could mistakenly be regarded as having been placed by
a private advertiser.
The co-operation of all concerned is much appreciated.
```

Exhibit 6.04
Typical notice found in classified columns

(c) *Mail Order Protection Scheme* — This is a voluntary scheme operated by many newspapers and magazines covering products and services advertised by them.

(d) *British Code of Advertising Practice* — This is another voluntary scheme to which most newspapers and magazines adhere. It states that most orders should be met within twenty-eight days.

6.8 *Direct Mail*

Leaflets/circulars are put through letter boxes inviting people to purchase such varied items as insurance, showers, central heating and double glazing. Anyone interested returns a prepaid card for more information.

Strictly this is not a direct method of selling, but it often used to provide salesmen with 'leads' (Details of people who may buy). The percentage of returned cards is very small (see also 16.17). How many of those delivered to your home are replied to?

6.9 *T.V. Sales*

Many low value items are advertised on T.V. inviting you to purchase direct from the distributor, e.g. records and cassettes.

6.10 *Telephone Selling*

Some organisations contact potential customers direct by telephone, this can cause annoyance to people who resent being disturbed at home.

42

6.11 Unethical methods

Over the last few years two methods of distribution have been legally curbed.

(a) *Inertia selling* — this occurs when, for example, a book which has not been ordered arrives through the post and subsequently a bill for it is sent. Many people won't bother to return the book — hence the use of the term inertia. Possibly it gets lost or damaged and since the cost rarely exceeds a few pounds some people would pay up to save further trouble.

Under the Unsolicited Goods and Services Act 1971 it is a criminal offence for a trader to ask for money for goods or services which he supplied but which were unasked for. Anything received in this way automatically becomes yours as a 'free gift' after six months unless you write to the sender asking him to collect it. In this case the sender has only thirty days in which to collect. After that time the goods become the property of the recipient.

(b) *Pyramid selling* — so called because one person bought the right to sell a product(s) or service(s) in a large area, i.e. a county. He sold the distribution rights for particular areas in the county, e.g. large towns to others. They in turn divided up 'their' towns or areas into smaller units, e.g. individual housing estates. In turn they sold the right to

Psst . . . Want to buy a pyramid?

distribute in that area to others who may have further subdivided 'their' estate into groups of streets which they would sell to those who would form the base of the pyramid. They would actually try to sell the product(s) or service(s).

Money was made from the right to sell the product rather than selling the product itself. Many people bought these rights to sell. Some people borrowed considerable sums of money to do so, and they incurred heavy losses.

The public was protected by the Fair Trading Act of 1973 which amongst other things made it an offence to take or ask for payment for recruiting others into a pyramid scheme. The Act also requires that anyone joining must receive a written contract setting out his/her rights.

6.12   *Exercise 2*

1   Account for the growth of mail order sales illustrated in 6.02.

2   Explain why goods offered for sale 'direct from manufacturer' may not be such a bargain.

3   Direct mail is comparatively cheap but has one major disadvantage. What is this?

4   What safeguards exist to protect people who buy goods through newspapers and magazines.

5   Under what circumstances can unordered goods be treated as 'free gifts'?

6.13   **Assignments**

1.   Using copies of newspapers and magazines provided, list twenty items advertised for sale, stating prices, newspaper or magazine in which item advertised, and whether or not direct from supplier.

2.   Draft an advertisement for inclusion in a newspaper asking for applicants for part-time mail order agents.

Chapter 7

Industrial Distribution

At the end of this chapter you should be able to:-

(A) Explain the nature and development of industrial distribution.

(B) Describe how industrial distribution satisfies the demands of its customers.

(C) Differentiate between various methods used to distribute goods and services.

(D) List the buying motives of industry.

(E) Describe how this sector of the industry differs from retail distribution.

7.1 *Nature and development*

Distribution serves two important groups of customers. These are individual retail customers and organisations. These include industrial and commercial businesses e.g. Leyland Cars, International Computers Ltd; Local Authority controlled undertakings e.g. local bus services; government departments e.g. The Ministry of the Environment; and Nationalised Industries e.g. The National Coal Board. The value of goods and services provided to these and other organisations runs into billions of pounds each year.

Just as retailing evolved to meet the needs of a growing and increasingly affluent consumer market, so industrial distribution has developed to meet the needs of organisational customers (mainly industrial).

These started to appear mainly as a result of the 'Industrial Revolution' which encouraged large scale productions and consumption. Industrial organisations and the complementary commercial and Government Organisations which supported them required goods and services in order to serve their customers.

Industry produces goods which can be divided into two types viz

(a) Producer goods — are required not because they are directly useful to people but because they can be used to make goods which people find useful and want, examples of producer goods are textile machinery, lathes and sheet metal.

(b) Consumer goods — are goods which are themselves useful to consumers either as individuals or organisations. Examples of consumer goods are clothing, carpets and cookers.

Sometimes it can be difficult to classify goods in this manner, they can be placed in either category depending on use. Thus ladders may be used in a factory as an aid in some manufacturing process (producer good) and in the home for a variety of reasons (consumer good).

The requirements of an organisation obviously depends on its size and functions, its needs are normally largely for producer goods which are provided by industrial distribution. An example of an early industrial organisation is a textile mill, it required in addition to a source of power only the raw material (wool), bought perhaps directly from the farmer or from the local wool exchange. It used a limited amount of relatively unsophisticated machinery bought from a few specialist manufacturers, together with spares and lubricants. This machinery would not require replacement either frequently or on a large scale.

Such an industrial organisation had only limited use for an industrial distribution network.

Contrast this with a modern major industrial organisation making cars for example. It requires materials e.g. sheet steel, copper wire and cloth; components e.g. lights, brakes and instruments, in addition to these are items which are not part of the car such administration items as stationery, computers, office equipment, and there are also jigs and tools and other machinery which are necessary to make the vehicles. A full list of all the items necessary to the full manufacturing processes involved in making cars would run into thousands of pages. The need for such a wide range of products in considerable quantities has encouraged the growth of a separate sector of distribution — Industrial Distribution.

7.2 Scope of industrial distribution

Industrial Distribution exists to meet the needs of every sector of industry and commerce. Some industrial distributors deal in goods which have a wide market e.g. office equipment and stationery; others will serve a more specialised market e.g. catering, motor vehicles or building.

Some industrial distribution networks serve overseas customers earning valuable foreign exchange.

Industrial distribution involves providing the same range of services provided by the wholesaler in the retailing sector i.e. breaking bulk, providing storage facilities, advice and credit (see 4.4).

7.3 Meeting the demands of industry and commerce

The role of industrial distribution is much the same as that of retail distribution — to satisfy its customers i.e. organisations. Remember this was expressed in Chapter Two in terms of the five rights:-

(a) Right price;   (d) Right time;
(b) Right quantity;   (e) Right goods;
(c) Right place;

(a) *Right price* — industrial buyers very often have to be very price conscious, since the price they pay for goods and services have in turn to be recovered from their customers. If their prices are higher than their competitors they risk losing sales, e.g. UK car manufacturers losing sales to imported cars.

(b) *Right quantity* — Industrial users may require goods in varying quantities from single items to many thousands e.g. brake shoes. Failure to supply the required quantity may cause the buying organisation a reduction in sales and additional costs. An industrial distributor will try to maintain a stock level sufficient to meet normal demands as would his counterpart in the retail sector.

(c) *Right place* — this is not so important as in retailing since less emphasis is placed on convenience.

(d) *Right time* — is very important if goods are being produced using a variety of processes and materials on a continuous basis. Should delivery of even one item be delayed then production can be seriously disrupted. This can lead to expensive shutdowns of production lines plus lost sales and lost reputation.

(e) *Right goods* — like the retailer, the industrial distributor must have merchandise which meets the needs of his customers if he is to remain in business. Many will wish to examine or test a number of products before ordering.

Users of industrial products may specify certain requirements e.g. ability to withstand certain temperatures. Industrial distributors have to take such factors into account in their efforts to meet the needs of their customers. As with failure to deliver on time, product defects can prove expensive for the buying organisation because of the resultant loss of sales and reputation and expensive repairs.

7.4 Methods of distribution

An industrial distributor may be the manufacturer distributing his own goods or an independent distributor who may distribute goods made by a number of competing manufacturers. The methods chosen will depend on a variety of factors such as the number of customers, the area covered, the nature of the goods and tradition but may involve:-

(a) *The trade counter* — this consists of a special area and/or a counter in a building occupied by an industrial distributor. An example of this is the trade counter in a builders merchants which serves many of the needs of local small scale builders. Sales assistants/warehouse staff obtain requested items, usually from stock. The customer normally requires a minimum of technical advice and obtains the items 'over the counter', although delivery may be arranged where necessary.

(b) *Representatives* — are used where the products being distributed are of a highly technical nature and/or are very expensive. The representative may act as a consultant advising potential clients on how the products he is selling can help solve the customers problems. The representative may have to make regular visits to advise the buyer regarding operation and maintenance.

(c) *Requests from the trade* — these may be placed orally e.g. over the telephone or in writing. Such requests may be to meet specific needs or they may be regular orders, e.g. from the purchasing department of a large organisation. These orders may arise from previous contacts, through trade exhibitions or other promotional activities, or possibly from tenders.

(d) *Direct from suppliers* — many organisations will not purchase their requirements through an independent distributor but will approach the supplier direct. This occurs when the buyer is in a position to place substantial and possibly regular orders. As a result of negotiating direct with the supplier and because of his purchasing power such a customer is able to obtain more favourable terms than by dealing with an intermediary. A large scale user of steel may thus deal direct with British Steel rather than with a steel stockist. The parallel in retailing is where the multiples and other large scale buyers deal direct with suppliers rather than making use of a wholesaler.

Another factor which encourages firms to deal directly with each other is the practice of offering special terms on a reciprocal basis. Thus an office equipment manufacturer may agree to buy the carpet he needs from a particular carpet manufacturer at a special price. In exchange the carpet manufacture buys this office equipment from the supplier also at a special price.

A customer may also deal direct with a manufacturer when buying a product designed solely to meet his needs.

7.5   *Exercise 1*

1. List one example of each type of organisation mentioned in 7.1 which would buy goods and services provided by industrial distribution.

2. Define and give one example of a producer good other than the one mentioned in the text.

3. What problems might a manufacturer encounter in trying to pass on the increased costs of components to his customers?

4. In each case give an example of a product which may be distributed in each of the following ways (a) over the trade counter (b) by representatives (c) requests from the trade (d) direct from manufacturer.

5. What would be the likely effects on the British car industry if Lucas, the manufacturer of vehicle electrical components, as a result of strikes, had to delay deliveries.

7.6 *Buying motives of customers*

It has been said that businesses and government agencies tend to buy goods and services on a more rational basis than most individual retail customers placing a large order. These large scale buyers will probably have considered the following points:-

(a) Price is very important but is by no means always the deciding factor. A large organisation may 'shop around' for the best price contacting a number of suppliers. Trade, quantity and cash discounts will all be considered.

(b) Reliability of supply is important because of the costs incurred if production delays occur.

(c) Quality should be such as to reduce to an acceptable minimum figure the number or quantity of defective products. For certain products quality needs to be such that ideally there are no defectives e.g. high pressure valves.

At worst, selling goods which fail or function imperfectly may endanger people's safety e.g. cars with defective components. In such cases the least damaging thing to happen is that the customer may be caused considerable trouble and expense. If defective products have to be recalled for rectification then this involves the maker in considerable trouble and expense. Obviously the manufacturer's reputation and sales of his product are affected.

An industrial or commercial buyer has the same basic problem as a retail customer such as a housewife. This is to purchase goods which meet the needs of the buyer or the final users, which would be her family in the case of the housewife. The retail customer requires goods of a certain quality and this is confirmed by the law in the Sale of Goods Act 1979. The industrial/commercial buyer is likely to be even more concerned with quality than the retail customer, since the consequences of poor quality are likely to be even more severe.

(d) Credit terms. The industrial/commercial organisation may have to extend credit to its customers and so may require in turn some form of credit from its own suppliers.

7.7 *Differences between industrial and retail distribution*

Whilst the two sectors of distribution, industrial and retail, have the same common purposes, i.e. providing their customers with the goods and services needed, they differ in a number of respects viz:-

(a) Virtually everyone purchases goods/services from the retailing sector. Much of industrial buying is in the hands of a small number of individuals, who in many instances are professional buyers.

(b) Many large organisations have found it advantageous to set up purchasing departments staffed by specialist buyers trained to make buying decisions.

(c) Retail customers may buy an article because it is new, or because they have seen it on television. Some purchases are made because the packaging is attractive. The industrial buyer tends to buy only after carefully considering the factors mentioned in 7.6.

(d) Industrial goods and services are usually promoted through the specialist and trade press, e.g. 'Construction News', rather than the more general advertising media used by retailing concerns such as television and national newspapers.

(e) Whilst there are fewer buyers than in the retail trade, the individual orders placed are much larger in money and quantity terms.

(f) Finance (credit), discounts and after sales service are usually more important than in the retail sector.

(g) There is a smaller number of outlets since much of the selling is done via representatives, buying departments or by direct contact with suppliers. The amenities provided by this sector are limited in contrast to the much better provision in retail outlets.

7.8 *Exercise 2*

1. Using an example of your own choice show what the likely consequences are of supplying defective materials/components.

2. What considerations may a 'rational' industrial buyer take into account in buying a car for his firm? Contrast this with the 'irrational' considerations in the minds of some individual retail customers.

3. List four items supplied by industrial distribution, where quality has to be of the very highest standard.

4. In what circumstances may a buyer deal directly with a supplier.

5. What benefits might accrue to an organisation which employs specialist purchasing staff.

7.9 Assignments

1. Take as an example a well known local or national industrial organisation, and list goods which they use and obtain from the industrial distribution sector.

2. Visit your local and/or college library and list ten periodicals or newspapers which might be consulted by industrial buyers. State selling points put forward in one advertisement from each periodical or newspaper.

Chapter 8

Hygiene

At the end of this chapter you should be able to:-

(A) Define hygiene.

(B) Explain the necessity for hygiene.

(C) List requirements for personal hygiene.

(D) Itemise areas in which shop and warehouse premises may be unhygienic.

(E) List the benefits which may accrue from hygiene consciousness.

8.1 *What is hygiene?*

Basically it is preventative medicine, i.e. it is a number of simple rules, most of which are common sense, which reduce your chances of either catching some disease and/or of passing it on to other people. These simple rules will only cost you a few minutes of your time each day, and a little forethought on your part.

Remember — anyone can, in certain circumstances, infect or be the cause of infecting others.

8.2 *Why is hygiene so important?*

(a) *Effects on personal health*

Poor attention to elementary hygiene rules can result in yourself and/or others getting food poisoning or dysentry. See exhibit 8.01.

The causes of food poisoning are tiny germs which are only visible when viewed through a microscope. These bacteria (germs) can either cause food poisoning or produce toxins (poisons). Germs can be spread in numerous ways:-

(i)   by animals — rats, mice, birds;

(ii) by people;

(iii) by dirty premises or equipment;

(iv) by contaminated food or utensils;

(v)   by air.

There are many types of food poisoning, some of which may cause only several hours of discomfort eg. slight nausea (feeling sick) and mild diarrhoea.

In more serious forms, food poisoning results in fever, severe vomiting, diarrhoea, stomach pains and cramps. In some cases it has caused death either directly or indirectly.

Obviously, no one would wish to be the cause of this, either to themselves or to others, when by being careful you can greatly reduce the risk.

Food poisoning in England, 1975*

Causative agent	General outbreaks		Family outbreaks		Sporadic cases notified or ascertained	Total No. of outbreaks and sporadic cases columns (1+3+5)	Total No. of cases columns (2+4+5)
	No. of separate outbreaks	No. of cases notified or ascertained	No. of separate outbreaks	No. of cases notified or ascertained			
	1	2	3	4	5	6	7
1. *Salmonella typhimurium*	42 (40)	594 (292)	229 (142)	589 (411)	1,107 (787)	1,378 (969)	2,290 (1,490)
2. Other salmonella	97 (55)	1,910 (860)	397 (210)	1,067 (534)	2,262 (1,192)	2,756 (1,457)	5,239 (2,586)
3. *Clostridium welchii*	41 (30)	1,441 (890)	11 (10)	95 (36)	35 (19)	87 (59)	1,571 (945)
4. *Staphylococcus aureus*	17 (6)	256 (86)	4 (4)	9 (14)	35 (31)	56 (41)	300 (131)
5. Other causes	7 (11)	41 (298)	16 (13)	39 (69)	63 (102)	86 (126)	143 (469)
6. Cause unknown	26 (42)	453 (421)	108 (138)	293 (421)	642 (832)	776 (1,012)	1,393 (1,674)
7. Totals	230 (184)	4,695 (2,847)	765 (517)	2,097 (1,485)	4,144 (2,963)	5,139 (3,664)	10,936 (7,295)

*Figures for 1974 in parenthesis.
Note:- These statistics relate only to reported cases. Actual cases would be higher.

Exhibit 8.01

(b) *Effects on shop and warehouse*

Poor standards of hygiene can affect a shop or warehouse or indeed most businesses in a number of ways, all of them adversely:

If the hygienic standards generally are low (e.g. dirty premises, machinery, counters and clothing) then this will deter people from shopping in that store. Moreover they will tell their friends and neighbours, thus the store will get a bad name or image. Nor does it do your image any good if you work there, particularly if you wish to apply for a job elsewhere.

This disregard for hygiene will result in fewer customers, lower sales and therefore less money to meet business expenses, which include your wages! Eventually if the business is not making sufficient profit for the owner he may close it down — and you are then out of a job.

The local environmental health inspector is likely to call, perhaps the call may be a routine visit or it may be the result of a complaint by one of your (ex) customers. The environmental health inspector, who works for the local authority, has the power to:—

(i)   require the store owner/manager to make small changes e.g. clean things up;

(ii) issue a condemnation notice — which means disposal of food considered unfit for human consumption;

(iii) in extreme cases, close down the business or part of it;

(iv) prosecute, should he decide to do so it would be under either:-
      (A) the Food Hygiene (General) Regulations 1970 under which the business can be fined up to £100 for each breach of the regulations. There is also the possibility of up to three months imprisonment for the responsible officials.

      (B) the Offices, Shops and Railway Premises Act 1963 which covers a number of areas closely related to hygiene e.g. overcrowding, cleanliness, ventilation and sanitation.

A court appearance is likely to prove time consuming and legal costs can be high. The greatest cost however will be bad publicity — quite possibly a report of the case will appear in the local paper with obvious effects on sales.

As a result of an outbreak of food poisoning which occurred in 1983 in Winlaton near Gateshead, two men died and ten other people were made seriously ill. Many shops in the area reported a fall in trade as frightened customers bought elsewhere.

In July 1978, four pensioners were infected by botulism, a severe form of food poisoning, as a result of eating tinned salmon. The deaths of two of the pensioners, and the national publicity given to the incident through the media, resulted, not only in the withdrawal of the affected type of salmon, but most other brands even though there was no question of them being contaminated.

(C) Finally, one of the relevant legal rules which applies here and in other situations is called "vicarious liability". Essentially this means that the law holds the employer liable for many of the mistakes made by his employees. Remember! ignorance of the law is no excuse.

Don't forget that these regulations apply to all people who handle open food at any stage in distribution.

8.3 *Exercise 1*

1. Define in your own words the term 'hygiene'
2. Give three symptoms of possible food poisoning.
3. What are likely to be the effects of poor hygiene on customers, on sales, and on the image of the business?
4. What powers does the environmental health inspector have?
5. Name the laws which relate to hygiene.

8.4 *Personal hygiene*

(a) Some things are obviously desirable, such as washing hands, not spitting and not smoking whilst handling or being near food.

(b) Cuts, which may contain harmful bacteria, should be covered with a waterproof dressing. Germs can be passed on, especially by someone who washes food or plates and cutlery which come into contact with the food. Note that washing in warm or hot water does not kill all types of germs.

(c) Anyone suffering form certain infections e.g. 'flu or a skin disease should stay at home. By going to work they are going to share their germs with others — staff and customers.

Another group of diseases is so serious that the occurence of them has to be reported to the medical officer of health, e.g. Typhoid and Smallpox.

(d) Toilets and washing facilities must be provided, and notices requesting staff to wash their hands after using them.

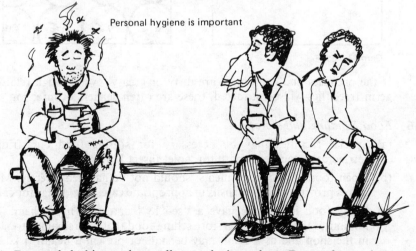

Personal hygiene is important

(e) Personal clothing and overalls must be kept clean. Do not forget that to many customers, you (the sales assistant), represent the store. The customer probably only comes into contact with you, and so may judge the store on your appearance, cleanliness and hygiene-consciousness.

8.5 *Premises*

It is no use having hygienic, well-scrubbed staff if the equipment and premises are dirty and unhygienic. They may be so for a variety of reasons. e.g.

(a) dirty or greasy floors and walls;

(b) dirty or greasy equipment;

(c) the presence of rats, mice and cockroaches which carry germs;

(d) badly heated and ventilated premises — this can encourage germs to multiply.

Under suitable conditions, germs multiply by dividing into two every 20-30 minutes. So one germ can become over 2 million in 7 hours. If you doubt the correctness of the arithmetic, try asking your lecturer in Business Calculations. He will be interested in this form of progression. After 12 hours continuous growth there may be 7 billion.

 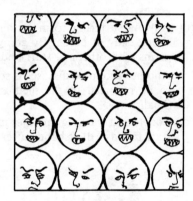

Germs breed

If the premises and equipment are dirty or greasy, even though relatively germ free, flies will be attracted, these are often carriers of infection.

8.6 *Food handling and storage*

(a) Special facilities may be necessary for storing food e.g. fridges, refrigerated counters and ultra violet insect killers;

(b) Open food, e.g. cooked meats, should not be handled directly. Many stores provide special utensils in appropriate cases, e.g. tongs for cakes;

(c) Many food items now have a "sell by" date shown on them. This minimises the chances of a store selling food that has remained too long in the shop and as a result may be stale or present a health risk. You should not sell these items after the date on the packet;

(d) As has already been mentioned, the preparation and storage of food is covered by the Food Hygiene (General) Regulations 1970 which are part of the Food and Drugs Act 1955.

8.7 *Benefits of hygiene consciousness*

(a) Unwashed floors, dirty cutlery, staff wearing grubby overalls may not in themselves result in food poisoning. However such obvious disregard indicates that the possibility exists. This will "put off" many would-be customers. It requires only a little time, attention and money to correct this impression.

(b) The benefits to business of hygiene precautions include:-

(i) extra custom;

(ii) reduction in the likelihood of customers, staff and others (e.g. deliverymen and representatives) contracting food poisoning;

(iii) reducing the possibility of prosecution and losses resulting from ii) above;

(iv) reduction in losses due to spoiled merchandise.

It thus makes good business sense to be hygiene conscious. The store owner(s) may spend money on advertising which would be wasted if poor hygiene conditions deter the customer from buying.

8.8 *Exercise 2*

1. Give three examples of how you personally can minimise the risk of passing on any infection.

2. For what reasons may premises and/or equipment be regarded as unhygienic?

3. What is meant by the term "sell by" date and why is it used?

4. What special facilities may be necessary for the handling and storage of food?

5. What benefits can a business achieve from careful attention to hygiene?

8.9 **Assignments**

1. As a manager of a store who has to give a brief talk to his staff on the importance of hygiene, make a brief plan of your proposed talk including precautions, risks involved and consequences.

2. Write an account of an imaginary court case involving a breach of the food hygiene regulations including:-
Prosecution — description of the offence;
    — how it came to light;
Defence — possible reasons why it happened;
Consequences — to business and to owner.

56

Chapter 9

Safety

At the end of this chapter you should be able to describe safety measures and practices and explain the need for them. In particular this means being able to:

(A) State the reasons why safety is important.

(B) Describe the situations in which people can be at risk.

(C) Outline the main provisions of the Offices, Shops and Railway Premises Act 1963.

(D) Outline the main provisions of the Health and Safety at Work Act 1974.

9.1 *How safe is distribution?*

The safer we can make the store the less chance there is of anyone, either customers or employees, being injured. Compared to many factories a shop is a reasonably safe place in which to be. Nevertheless, each year several people who work in the distributive trades are killed and many more are injured. See exhibits 9.01 and 9.02.

	Number of Fatal Accidents					
	1976	1977	1978	1979	1980	19*
Mining and Quarrying	88	66	82	79	71	
Textiles	3	3	4	3	3	
Electrical Engineering	6	7	6	8	7	
Chemicals	10	21	17	16	9	
Construction	143	138	122	129	122	
Distributive Trades	**45**	**56**	**46**	**43**	**37**	

Source: Health and Safety Statistics 1980. H.M.S.O.
*Student to enter latest figures.

Exhibit 9.01
Comparison of fatal accidents in selected industry sectors

9.2 *Why should we be safety conscious?*

There are three reasons why each of us, no matter who we are, should try to make our surroundings — at home, work or elsewhere, as safe as possible.

Accident classification	Retail shops	Wholesale departments warehouses
Machinery:		
Non-power machinery in motion	96	38
Machinery in motion under power	288	125
Machinery (or relevant part) at rest	160	143
Total machinery accidents	544	306
Transport:		
Vehicle in motion not moved by power	224	144
Vehicle moved by power	88	376
Vehicle stationary	100	256
Total transport accidents	412	776
Falls of persons:		
On or from fixed stairs	554	126
On or from ladders	185	123
Other falls from one level to another	324	345
Falls on the same level	1,131	507
Total falls of persons	2,194	1,101
Stepping on or striking against objects or persons	606	295
Handling goods (not elsewhere specified)	2,180	1,803
Struck by falling objects	597	333
Fires and explosions	17	9
Due to electricity	36	10
Use of hand tools	865	137
Other accidents	535	292
Total reported accidents	7,986	5,063
Fatal accidents	5	6

Source: Health and Safety Executive

Exhibit 9.02
Offices, Shops and Railway Premises Act: Total number of reported accidents occuring in Retail and Wholesale Premises 1980

(a) *Ethical* — Any reasonable person would think we owed it to others not to do anything or fail to do anything reasonable in order to reduce accidents. 'Do unto others as you would wish they would do unto you'.

(b) *Legal* — the law, both criminal and civil, also states that you should take care to reduce safety hazards. It penalises those who fail to do so, when injury occurs. This is discussed in more detail later (see 9.6).

(c) *Financial* — The high money costs of accidents (see 9.3), in addition to the pain and discomfort, cannot be overlooked.

9.3 *What accidents cost*

(a) *Cost to Society* — The costs of medical treatment, hospitals, ambulances and medicines resulting from accidents are paid by society in general, but chiefly by a group of which you are a member, that is of wage or salary earners. These costs are met from income tax and other forms of taxation. Each pay day among the deductions from your wage or salary is one for National Health Contributions.

There is also the far greater cost of lost work. Someone off sick for a week obviously cannot do his job. Therefore the store and the community lose the value of that person's normal work.

According to the Department of Health and Social Security, between 1972 and 1978 the number of days lost due to industrial accidents occurring in the distributive trades, for which medical certificates were issued, averaged 1,200,000 per year. If we take the average cost for each day of lost work as being £20 then the figure for the year is £24,000,000. The actual cost to society is probably greatly in excess of this figure.

The state pays sickness and other related benefits to those who have had accidents. The cost of these is ultimately met by the taxpayer — you!

Under the National Insurance (Industrial Injuries) Act 1965, all persons in insurable employment are insured against:

(i) Personal injury caused by accident arising out of an in the course of their employment.

(ii) Certain diseases and personal injuries not caused by accident but which are due to the nature of the persons' employment.

(b) *Costs to the Business* — As well as losing the benefit of the injured person's work, the business may also have to pay him. If the injury resulted from the negligence of the store then the injured person, whether employee, customer or anyone else, can sue the store. This may mean heavy legal costs and compensation, which can be thousands of pounds in a case where someone is seriously injured.

This incidentally is why businesses are compelled by law to have insurance to cover these possibilities, known as employers' liability insurance. Otherwise they may not be in a position to pay compensation to the injured.

(c) *Costs to the Individual* — No-one can put a price on the suffering and loss of enjoyment resulting from an accident. Certain results can be costed, e.g. loss of earnings and damage to clothes and to other personal possessions.

9.4 *Who is at risk?*

(a) *The customer* — can be at risk because of our lack of care in the faulty stacking of goods, greasy or slipper floors and cluttered gangways. Such cases can cost the store a great deal of money — legal fees, compensation and adverse publicity.

(b) *The staff* — can be at risk in a variety of situations, such as using dangerous equipment, e.g. food slicing machines — which cause about one third of all reported accidents occurring in shops.

(c) *Others* — such as representatives and deliverymen, who may be put at risk by lack of care in the stockrooms and delivery bays due to poor lighting, unauthorised use of equipment by untrained personnel and uneven and/or slippery floors.

In addition inadequate fire equipment and precautions, lack of emergency exits, poor lighting, lack of appropriate training and first aid facilities, affect the safety of all.

9.5 *Exercise 1*

1. Imagine an accident and state what costs might follow from this accident and who would pay for them.
2. Using the exhibits provided state which are the four major causes of reported accidents in a) Retail Shops, b) Warehouses.
3. Which risks are workers insured against under the National Insurance (Industrial Injuries) Act 1965?
4. What is Employers' Liability Insurance and why is it compulsory by law.
5. Give four examples of potential hazards in the store.

9.6 *The Law*

The law protects people from safety hazards and in some cases even from themselves. If it were not for the law many people would probably ignore safety considerations and the number of accidents and deaths would be higher than it is.

(a) *Civil Law* — The civil law is concerned with the rights of the individual and the actions of others who affect these rights. If as an individual you do something or fail to do something which interferes with another person's rights, then you may have committed a 'tort' (a Civil Law wrong).

Everyone has a legal right to expect others to take reasonable care in their business and other activities so that people are not put at risk.

Anyone who behaves carelessly may be breaking this duty of care rule. This tort is called 'negligence' and anyone taken to court in such circumstances and who is found guilty may have to pay a great deal of compensation.

(b) *Criminal Law* — Basically a criminal act is one which can harm any individual citizen, in certain circumstances negligence may be a criminal offence.

The principal laws concerned with safety are:-

(i) The Offices, Shops and Railway Premises Act 1963

(ii) The Health and Safety at Work Act 1974.

The Offices, Shops and Railway Premises Act 1963 regulates working conditions in premises covered by this Act. Many of the provisions of this act relate directly or indirectly to safety such as:

(i)   A room in which people work must not be so overcrowded as to cause risk of injury to health.

(ii) Lighting should be suitable and sufficient.

(iii) Floors, passages and stairs should be kept as free as is reasonably practicable from obstruction and from slippery substances. Stairs must have handrails.

(iv) Guards are required on dangerous parts of machinery.

(v)   Only those over 18 and suitably trained may clean certain machinery.

(vi) Restrictions on lifting or moving heavy weights.

(vii) Providing adequate first aid facilities.

(viii) Imposing penalties for dangerous acts and interference with equipment.

(ix) Fire precautions.

The Health and Safety at Work Act 1974 relates to any type of workplace and requires that the employer ensures, so far as is reasonably practicable, that the health, safety and welfare of employees and others is looked after.

"Reasonably practicable" means what a reasonable man would do to limit hazards, e.g. a reasonable man would make sure that there were enough fire doors fitted. This does not mean that it would be reasonably practicable to expect him to replace all doors with fire doors.

The employer's duties under this act are to:-

(i) Draw up and publish a safety policy statement;

(ii) Ensure that safety procedures are carried out;

(iii) Keep and publish safety records;

(iv) Advise staff and others of their responsibilities; in other words to promote and maintain safe working conditions.

Employees are also held responsible by law if they do not follow safe methods of working.

The Health and Safety Executive or enforcing authority, i.e. local inspector of the Environmental Health Department may prohibit the use of unsafe machinery or premises, and may institute criminal proceedings against those who break the law.

Under the Act either the employer or employee may be fined an unlimited amount. Additionally a gaol sentence of up to two years can be imposed in extreme cases.

9.7 Exercise 2

1. Define negligent behaviour and give one example of such behaviour.

2. State four provisions of the Offices, Shops and Railway Premises Act 1963 which relate to safety.

3. State in your own words what "reasonably practicable" means.

4. What duties have been imposed on employers by the Health and Safety at Work Act 1974?

5. What penalties may be imposed on those who break this law?

9.8 Assignments

1. Make a list of ten areas/items you would look at if asked to do a safety check in your store.

2. A colleague makes the following statement "Think of the money spent on safety precautions in this store. It's not necessary. Nobody's ever been injured here — a waste of time and money." How would you convince him otherwise? (essay)

62

Chapter 10

Organisation in a Distributive Firm

At the end of this chapter you should be able to:-
(A) Describe the different levels of management.
(B) Explain their functions.
(C) List supporting services.
(D) Identify their roles.

10.1 *The need for management*

The management of any business involves dealing with a range of problems. Their size and variety obviously varies with the nature of the business and its size. In large organisations, such as department stores or multiples, these problem areas are often sufficient to justify the appointment of a specialist manager or department to deal with them.

Such problem areas can include personnel, finance, training, office services, display and advertising, transport, warehousing and security. Sometimes two or more of these areas may be grouped together because of their close relationship with one another such as training and personnel.

Many small retail businesses have an owner/manager (as is the case with cornershops). In these businesses the problems which arise are dealt with, in the main, by the owner. In certain instances he may call for professional advice from solicitors and accountants. Usually the problems are not so serious as to require the services of an expert, but can often be solved by the owner drawing on his own experience.

10.2 *Classification of management*

In large scale businesses, including retail organisations, a group of people is required to organise and run (manage) the business. These people (management) can be classified in a number of ways:-

  (a) line management;
  (b) staff management;
  (c) functional management;

(a) *Line management* — involves those managers who are directly concerned with the selling of the goods. Store managers, floor managers and department managers (buyers) are examples of this type. The lower levels of management e.g. the supervisory grades, are also in this group. Line management is so called because each person is responsible to the person above him in the chain or line of authority. (See exhibit 10.01)

(b) *Staff management* — involves those managers who are not directly concerned with the selling of the goods. Staff management may include people employed as personal assistants to senior managers, including directors, advisers on some particular aspect of the business, e.g. training officer advising warehousing department on courses and training methods. Note that these managers are advisers and have no direct responsibility for the department they advise.

(c) *Functional management* — involves those managers who are responsible for a particular function or area of business e.g. personnel, marketing or transport. Some of these are supporting services (see 10.5). Often such managers can also be classified as staff management (see (b) above). In practice, the distinctions between the different types of management are often blurred. Where the distinction is most clearcut is in multiples. Here the individual store management is line management because it is directly concerned with selling the goods and having a clear chain or line of command. The head office management group in a multiple consists mainly of staff/functional managers. These individuals are not directly involved in selling the goods e.g. training managers, industrial relations managers and accountants.

0.3 *Structure of management*

The basic structure of management is hierarchical or pyramid shaped. Each manager is responsible for those below him and in turn responsible to those above him. A typical store would be organised thus: See exhibit 10.01

Exhibit 10.01
Typical Store organisation

In this structure there are a number of levels or 'layers' of management. The number will vary according to the type of organisation. A cornershop will probably have only one i.e. the owner/manager who will probably have one or more fulltime or part-time assistants.

A retail business, which is organised as a company and has a large number of branches, or large store will probably be organised as follows: See exhibit 10.02.

64

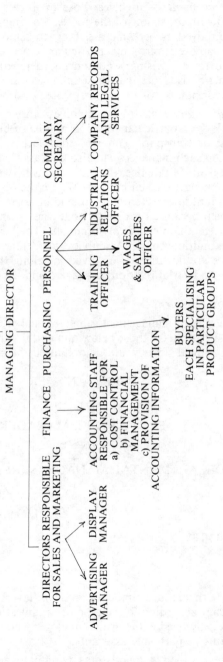

Exhibit 10.02
Simple organisation chart showing how a retail business
organised as a company may be structured

CHAIRMAN

MANAGING DIRECTOR

FINANCE   PURCHASING   PERSONNEL   COMPANY
SECRETARY

DIRECTORS RESPONSIBLE
FOR SALES AND MARKETING

ADVERTISING   DISPLAY
MANAGER   MANAGER

ACCOUNTING STAFF
RESPONSIBLE FOR
a) COST CONTROL
b) FINANCIAL
MANAGEMENT
c) PROVISION OF
ACCOUNTING INFORMATION

BUYERS
EACH SPECIALISING
IN PARTICULAR
PRODUCT GROUPS

TRAINING
OFFICER

WAGES
& SALARIES
OFFICER

INDUSTRIAL
RELATIONS
OFFICER

COMPANY RECORDS
AND LEGAL
SERVICES

This list is by no means exhaustive. A retail company involved in setting up new stores and reorganising existing ones may have a director concerned solely with store acquisition and planning.

One of the most important jobs done by directors is to make 'company policy'. This means they decide what the business should be trying to do. They then examine ways in which these objectives can be met. This might be a policy of expansion and examining areas in which expansion can take place.

Below the directors is the senior management level which can include area or regional managers and possibly the managers of large stores.

Middle management usually consists of departmental and floor managers. The managers of smaller units are also in this category. They carry out the policy decisions which have been taken. The lowest level is junior management. This includes the various supervisory grades and section heads who work within strict limits and procedures laid down by higher levels of management. The nature of the responsibilities of each of these levels of management will obviously depend on the organisation. Some indications of these can be obtained by examining job descriptions and job advertisements.

10.4 *Exercise 1*

1. Name four business problem areas and a specific problem relating to each area.
2. Define and give one example of line, staff and functional management.
3. The basic structure of management is pyramid shaped and based on a hierarchy of levels. Suggest why this is so.
4. Suggest one example of policy making, other than the one mentioned in the text, with which a board of directors might be concerned.
5. Why might the duties and responsibilities of one store manager differ from those of another who works for a different organisation?

10.5 *The range of supporting services*

There is a range of services which a distribution organisation can use, e.g. personnel, training, office services, display, transport and security. The extent to which these services are provided depends on the size and type of organisation — a small cornershop requires less than a department store. The presentation and organisation of these services will also be influenced by the type of business. Thus, display in a supermarket will differ from display in the mail order business.

(a) *Personnel*

This is a very important service and growing in importance each year. Basically, the personnel function involves dealing with employees. Its importance arises because:-

Firstly, a retailer's staff, particularly his sales staff, are people who are going to make a major contribution to efficiency and profitability. It is therefore advisable to:-

(i) select staff carefully;

(ii) encourage feelings of loyalty and commitment to the business. These are often fostered by the provision of welfare facilities and fringe benefits, such as social clubs, staff outings and pension schemes;

(iii) operate systems designed to aid management in decisions on promotions and regrading;

Secondly, a sound wage and salary structure is essential to maintain staff morale and co-operation. In retailing basic minimum rates are laid down by wages councils, 'covering' most of those who work in distribution and related trades. However a wage and salary structure needs to take into account the following:-

(i) Should the organisation pay above the minimum rates and if so by how much?

(ii) Should the store use some method of incentive payment, e.g. commission on sales, and how should this be calculated?

Thirdly, the industry for a number of reasons traditionally has had a low proportion of its members in trades unions. The Union of Shop, Distributive and Allied Trades (USDAW) is the main union. This may not always remain the case. However, the management will still have to discuss and settle pay and other conditions of employment with staff, irrespective of whether or not they belong to a union.

Finally, the law relating to employer/employee relationships has grown considerably in recent years. Pay and conditions; redundancy payments for those who lose their jobs; providing protection against unfair dismissal; obliging employers to provide safe working conditions; and prohibiting discrimination on certain grounds (e.g. race, creed, colour, and sex) are all now regulated by law.

Disclosure of information to employees and employee participation in management are two areas of possible future legislation.

This growth in the law has been accompanied by an increasing awareness amongst employees of their legal rights. Employers who operate in ignorance of these laws and their implications may find they have broken the law and have to pay the required penalty.

(b) *Training*

Education and training helps the individual employees to:-

(i) develop his skills and knowledge;

(ii) prepare himself for other tasks;

(iii) prepare himself for promotion;

(iv) develop job satisfaction;

It also helps the employer in the following ways:-

(i) ensures a steady flow of people with the necessary skills and knowledge for specific jobs;

(ii) reduces the likelihood of the employer failing to make use of, or losing, the services of able people;

(iii) enables the employer to meet his legal obligations in such areas as health, hygiene and safety;

(iv) increase sales and profitability as a result of better trained and educated staff.

Education and training can be in the form of in-store training which ranges from the informal e.g. being shown how to do a job by a colleague or manager, to the more formal organised training sessions.

Further education, much of it with a vocational bias, can be obtained from the many colleges and polytechnics. These offer a wide variety of courses which range from basic courses (such as your course) up to degree level in some instances.

(c) *Office services* (see also 11.1 onwards)

In order for any business, other than a very small one, to survive it needs to store, retrieve and send out information. Most of this information is in a written form such as letters, memos, price lists and catalogues. Office services, such as typing, duplications and filing, ensure that this information, necessary to the successful running of the business, is available. It is needed by management for a variety of reasons:-

(i) making decision, e.g. on buying and pricing;

(ii) assessing profitability;

(iii) analysing sales figures;

(iv) stocktaking and ordering;

(v) credit control.

For certain sections of the industry these services are more important than others e.g. mail order. Many distribution organisations now make use of computers to store, produce and interpret some of this information.

(d) *Display* (see also 17 onwards)

This is a very important service. It is no use having the right goods, at the right price and so on, a well laid out, well decorated store, staffed by courteous, knowledgeable and helpful sales assistants, if potential customers don't know this! Display is one method of making the customer aware of the store and its merchandise.

The larger stores will have a display department or section staffed by people who have specialist training in display.

Other stores, particularly chain stores, may have a specialist display unit centrally based, who tour the various branches. In other stores display may be left to untrained staff who may lack ability or flair. The preparation of display material, layouts and themes may be done centrally so the disadvantages of a lack of display staff are minimised.

(e) *Transport*

Transport is needed for goods coming into and going out of the store. In the former case, goods will be transported by the suppliers' own vehicles or by commercial carriers such as British Road Services. Some retailers may need their own transport, e.g. to visit a cash and carry warehouse.

In the other case, transport may be an essential supporting service without which sales would be seriously affected. Stores selling bulky and/or heavy merchandise such as furniture are expected to provide this service. Some stores provide a free delivery service while others may charge. The cost to the customer may vary according to:-

(i) the value of the goods ordered;

(ii) the distance involved;

Stores which offer a delivery service usually have their own delivery vehicles painted in the store's colours and showing the firm's name, thus providing additional advertising.

Another consideration for some customers is the social status reflected when the firm's delivery van stops outside their home.

(f) *Security*

With the heavy and increasing losses which stores incur as a result of theft, security is playing an increasingly important role.

It does not matter greatly who organises the security precautions, store personnel or an outside agency, what matters is that they exist if losses are to be minimised. These may arise in any of the following ways:-

(i) Theft by customers, staff and others. The theft of goods results in the loss of expected profit on the stolen goods and their cost. Narrow profit margins may mean that the loss of one item from a case can result in no profit being made on the sale of the caseload. Theft by the staff may also involve the loss of cash from tills.

These thefts can range from petty thefts undertaken inpulsively to systematic, well organised expeditions. Losses may then range from a few pounds to many thousands. The methods used to commit these thefts vary from the simple to the highly complex.

Losses due to theft by staff and others such as deliverymen and representatives are arguably greater than those due to customers because of their greater knowledge and opportunity.

(ii) Damage to premises. The principal type of risk here is from fire. Various detection systems and control apparatus can be installed such as heat or smoke sensitive alarms, sprinkler systems and fire extinguishers.

(iii) Loss of cash in transit. This occurs particularly when taking it from the store to the bank or post office.

Security, in addition to trying to minimise losses due to the above, can also have a role in reducing losses due to poor handling and storage, e.g. losses due to pest infestation.

Good security precautions and staff (either the firms' own or those of an outside agency) should in many instances make a substantial contribution to offsetting their cost by reducing losses and deterring potential thieves.

10.6   *Exercise 2*

1. What factors might a personnel department consider in fixing wage and salary levels?

2. "Training is largely a waste of money, what you need to know you'll pick up as you go along". Comment on this statement.

3. List four retail organisations in your area which deliver goods and state what merchandise they supply.

4. How may a retailer recover the money he spends on security? Give examples.

5. How may the lack of trained display personnel be compensated for?

10.7   **Assignments**

1. Using, if necessary, appropriate existing advertisements and job descriptions, draw up an advertisement for a senior management position in the distributive trades.

2. Complete the given chart, adding you own example.

Chapter 11

Documentation

At the end of this Chapter you should be able to:-
(A) List and describe the essential documents used in buying and selling transactions paying particular attention to the order, invoice, credit note, debit note, statement, and methods of settlement.

It is essential in the running of an efficient and profitable business to control the buying, selling and pricing of stock. Too much stock will 'tie up' unnecessary capital which could be used for other purposes. On the other hand, too little stock will lead to shortages and loss of customers who will buy elsewhere. Before examining these problems more closely, we must look at the stages in a transaction between buyer and supplier. For any new business the first task is to buy stock from which to sell. In established businesses the buying of new merchandise is controlled by the amount of goods still in stock and anticipated demand.

11.1 *Documentation*

The following can be regarded as the major stages in a transaction between buyer and seller. This is not common to all businesses as some prefer to adopt their own system.

(a) *Enquiry*

This is a request by a retailer to a manufacturer or supplier for a copy of their price list or catalogue.

(b) *Price List or Catalogue*

This will be sent by the supplier. It contains a full description of the goods, prices, conditions of sale, terms, discounts, mode of carriage, minimum orders, special offers, returns procedure and any other information relevant to the buyer's needs.

A catalogue will also provide photographs of the goods to be supplied. As they are expensive to produce, a manufacturer normally has only two editions printed each year. In addition to photographs the catalogue will contain information as to sizes and ranges of goods available. It will be sent out together with a price list which is cheaper to prepare and can be up-dated at very little extra cost.

(c) *Order*

After deciding how and what to order the appropriate form is completed. Included on the order form should be details such as price, description, catalogue or price list number, quantity, where to send goods to, and any other special delivery instructions. It often occurs that the address for delivery differs from the address on the order. Attention must be drawn to this.

The actual writing of an order is unnecessary in quite a few cases as suppliers send representatives. They make regular visits, take the order, and try to ensure that special instructions are carried out. In some buying organisations Head Office permission is required prior to purchase. A Purchase Requisition Note then has to be made out prior to ordering. This informs the buying office or Head Office that goods are required. In many cases goods cannot be bought, by a manager, without the approval of senior management.

One obvious reason for this is the negotiation of special discounts for large bulk orders which are made by Head Office for delivery to branches. These are often know as allocations.

(d) *Acknowledgement*

This is sent by the supplier to the buyer acknowledging receipt of order.

(e) *Advice Note*

This informs the buyer that the goods have been despatched and gives details of the method of transport.

(f) *Delivery Note*

This accompanies the goods and enables the buyer to check them off. It is often a carbon copy of the invoice. Some organisations at this stage require an internal document, known as a Goods Received Note, to be completed. It contains the name and address of the supplier, date, number of cases or articles received, shortages, any damage and the condition of the goods.

(g) *Invoice*

The invoice is sent after delivery. This is the document which stipulates the price of goods bought and the total amount spent. It contains details of purchases, quantities, unit price, total price, discounts, terms for prompt payment and VAT. Invoices should be checked thoroughly to ensure correct prices have been charged, and accurate calculations have been made.

(h) *Credit Note*

A credit note, which is usually printed in red, will be sent to the buyer for any of the following reasons:-

(i) goods have been overcharged e.g. incorrect price on invoice or incorrect additions and calculations creating an overcharge.

(ii) goods have been returned e.g. damaged, inferior goods sent as substitutes; items included in delivery but not ordered; returns for bottles, empties, cases, or gift vouchers.

(iii) cancellation of the invoice.

The value of a credit note reduces the amount owing by the buyer in the accounts of the seller.

(j) *Debit Note*

This is the opposite of the credit note and is sent to the buyer for any of the following reasons:-

(i) more goods were sent than had been invoiced and they have been retained by the buyer.

(ii) goods have been undercharged, e.g. wrong price quoted on invoice or incorrect addition creating an undercharge.

(iii) goods supplied were of higher quality (and therefore of higher price) than those stipulated on the invoice and have been retained by the buyer.

(iv) any ommissions from the invoice e.g. items delivered but not included.

The value of a debit note increases the amount owing by the buyer in the accounts of the seller.

(k) *Statement*

This is sent out at the end of a trading period, usually at monthly intervals. It gives details of:-

(i) amounts purchased in that period;

(ii) any adjustments e.g. credit or debit notes;

(iii) any discounts received;

(iv) balance from previous statement (if any);

(v) payments received from the buyer during the month (if any)

The final most important figure is the amount which the buyer owes the seller who is now asking to be paid. In practice most buyers wait for the statement before paying and do not pay each individual invoice as it arrives.

(l) *Settlement*

The amount on the statement is paid either by cheque, Giro, postal order, money order or cash.

(m) *Receipt*

This is issued by the seller acknowledging payment of the amount owing. It shows the details of amount paid, how paid, date, and it is signed by an official of the company e.g. cashier. If payment is made by cheque, then no receipt is necessary. In many cases firms still continue to issue receipts as an additional check against fraud.

11.2 *Exercise 1*

1. List the major documents used in a business transaction of buying and selling.

2. Give reasons why a credit note is issued.

3. Give reasons why a debit note is issued.

11.3   Assignments

1. After obtaining permission, collect samples of the documents handled in your own store and explain why they are used. They must include those sent by suppliers, and those your store sends with orders.

2. Using the following details, complete the blank invoice provided by the teacher:-

    1 white shade @ £2.00, 1 wall clock @ £9.00, 2 wall brackets @ £1.50 each, 5 one way switches @ £2.75 each, add VAT at the rate of 15%.

    Use imaginary names and addresses for the supplier and the customer.

Chapter 12

Warehouse Stock

At the end of this Chapter you should be able to:-
(A) Explain the need for checking incoming goods.
(B) Describe an effective checking procedure.
(C) List the details required in a goods received book.
(D) List the essentials of a good storage area.
(E) Explain the need for careful stock control.
(F) Identify the problems related to the handling and care of goods.
(G) Explain the need for stock rotation.
(H) Explain the need for security of goods in stock.

12.1 *Goods received procedure*

This is a very important part of the work of any retail organisation. The checking of goods cannot be left to an inexperienced person. It must be done thoroughly and accurately. Profit calculations can largely depend on the amount of goods ordered and paid for being received into the shop. The loss of one case will have to be deducted from the profit made on the remainder. In these days of reduced profit margins the loss of one case can eliminate the profit on all the others.

(a) *Checking procedure.*

    (i) A quick glance at the condition of the consignment as it is off-loaded will be of great importance. Look for signs of loose flaps on boxes or cases and also for cut wires. These indicate possible pilfering. Examine badly damaged parcels or wet patches caused by rain. All these affect the condition of the goods.

    (ii) Count the items and make sure they correspond with the delivery note. Carriers such as British Rail will only require a signature for a specified number of parcels. The contents are of no importance to them, and they must therefore be checked against documentation sent by the supplier.

    (iii) Check that the order numbers correspond to those which have been issued for that particular delivery. Many retail organisations allot an order number to each supplier for ease of identification. This highlights wrong deliveries, especially between branches. Each separate branch will have its own particular prefix to an order number e.g. 01 London, 02 Birmingham, 03 Leeds.

(iv) Many suppliers allot a consignment number to each delivery. This number is marked on all the cases. Make sure these numbers are all the same and correspond to the delivery note.

(v) In addition to looking for shortages or damaged goods, it is important to look for duplications i.e. more items delivered than were ordered. It is easier to return them at the time of delivery than to arrange transport to pick them up at a later date.

There are two important methods of checking goods:-

(vi) *Direct Check*

Here the goods are checked against either the invoice or delivery note. This is a very accurate method and one adopted by most organisations. Where parcels contain mixed items it is easier to unpack all the items before checking. Another useful tip is to put the checked goods on to a cart or pallet for subsequent transfer to the stock room.

(vii) *Random Check*

This method can only be used for a consignment of goods which are identical. If the number of cases is correct then a random sample is taken throughout the delivery. If this sample appears to be as specified, then it can be assumed that the whole delivery is as specified. An example where this is used would be to check a consignment of bulk tea or coffee which has been bought by sample and quality. Remember the Sale of Goods Act 1979. See also 15.5

12.2 Goods Received Book

It is useful to have a Goods Received Book which records each delivery as it is received into the store. At a later date this book can be referred to in case of queries. Some or all of the following details should be entered into it:-

(a) date;

(b) supplier;

(c) consignment number;

(d) order number;

(e) number of packages;

(f) carrier;

(g) condition.

Remember at all times when signing for goods received to ensure that they correspond with the documentation. When in doubt sign for them as 'damaged', 'short delivered' or 'unchecked'.

12.3 *Storing*

(a) In order to reduce future wastage it is essential that the goods are stored correctly. Proper stock rotation should be carried out to ensure that the old stock is used first. This is essential for both food and non-food items. Food quickly deteriorates and all perishables are date coded, after which they should be withdrawn from sale. See also 8.6c. In the case of non-food items such as fashions, change is quick, Spring fashions cannot be sold in the Summer except at reduced prices.

(b) Remember to use the two principles of:-

(i) first in, first out (FIFO) *or*

(ii) last in, last out (LILO)

(c) Characteristics of a Storage Area. (See also 8.6.) When choosing a storage area it must be: –

(i) neat, clean, tidy and well illuminated;

(ii) dry and free from damp or leaking roofs;

(iii) kept free of direct sunlight. Either have no windows in the stock room or cover them during Summer. Materials quickly fade and many goods deteriorate in direct sunlight.

(iv) adequately ventilated. A constant change of air is essential to prevent stagnation. Large warehouses can have doors at either end to create a through draught. Small stock rooms often have extractor fans to draw out the air.

(v) at the correct temperature e.g. perishables and frozen food require to be refrigerated. There must be enough warmth to prevent condensation in wet weather.

(vi) supplied with strong shelving to eliminate stacking goods on top of each other. Batches can be segregated and it makes it easier to store small or specialised items.

(vii) have wide aisles, free from loose items. This enables the staff to stack goods or easily remove them for use in the store. Clear aisles are essential when using mechanical devices such as fork lift trucks.

(viii) free from pest infestation. Regular checks by organisations experienced in this field will control pests. It is extremely difficult in large warehouses to eliminate them entirely.

(d) Remember not to stack heavy items on light items or large goods on small goods. The more that can be put on the shop floor, the more room there will be in the warehouse. Goods do not sell in the warehouse where they cannot be seen.

(e) Organise the stock room and leave adequate space for deliveries. Try and keep items in the same space where the staff know where to find them. Fast selling and heavy items should be kept in a convenient place, near the door if possible for easy access. Where cases are coded or printed ensure that the face bearing the coding/printing is towards the front. If it does not, mark the case with its contents. Do not mix deliveries. Keep them separate to ensure proper stock rotation.

(f) Material picks up dust very easily and becomes soiled. Ensure any material is adequately covered by polythene. The same applies to other goods which must be kept dust free.

If the storage area is properly organised:-

(i) the stock will be easier to find;

(ii) it will take less time to check the stock;

(iii) items will not be overlooked.

2.4 *Exercise 1*

1. Outline the method your store uses to check incoming goods. Be prepared to discuss your method with other members of the group.

2. Design a layout which could be used in a Goods Received Book.

3. Why is stock rotation necessary?

2.5 *Stock control*

Effective stock control improves the profitability of any retail organisation. Regular stock checks can produce very useful information regarding

(a) *Which 'lines' to stock.*

These are usually the fast selling 'lines' always in demand and need ordering frequently. A business based on popular fast selling lines will be more successful than one with a large proportion of slow sellers.

(b) *Which lines to 'drop'.*

These are the slow sellers not in great demand by the customers. They lower the selling efficiency of a store and need eliminating. Care must be taken when deciding which lines to stop selling. Even slow sellers attract certain customers e.g. specialist lines. Many command a higher profit margin e.g. preserves containing liqueur. Do not cut out all the slow selling lines at the same time. Experiment until there is a noticeable drop in turnover. Never be afraid to put back an item which was considered to be a poor seller if its elimination has had an overall drastic effect on turnover. Always remember that related sales will increase the turnover. See also 13.3d.

(c) *How much to order.*

Careful stock control can ensure that just enough stock is held to carry over until the next delivery. This ensures regular supplies of new stock, and stops the danger of items becoming shop soiled. It also reduces the amount of money 'tied up' in stock.

(d) *Frequency of ordering*

In many cases the frequency of ordering depends on how often the representative calls. For fast selling lines it can be at three to five day intervals.

Moderate 'sellers' can be ordered every two to three weeks. Slow sellers will probably be ordered every four to six weeks. Seasonal lines e.g. Easter Eggs or Christmas specialities only require ordering once a year.

(e) *Which lines to promote and which to change.*

The promotion of different 'lines' varies from store to store. It is not always sound policy to promote fast selling lines. Less popular lines can improve with a boost from advertising or from being sited in a prime selling area. New lines are often slow sellers but can eventually become household names. There are occasions when a new line exceeds demand but later becomes a poor seller and has to be dropped.

A wide range of products is produced by many manufacturers. A slow line of one particular brand can be improved by changing to a more popular brand. Take note of regional demands. Large items e.g. washers, cookers or refrigerators require very little effort to control. This can be done visually. They are either there or they are not there. Watch delivery dates to ensure enough back up stock is arriving.

Items contained in stands e.g. batteries or cassettes can clearly be seen when stocks are getting low. Fast selling lines are those which require constant re-ordering.

Other items will require some form of documentation either in the form of a book or record card. An elaborate system is not needed but the available information should include:-

(i) Name and address of manufacturer or supplier;

(ii) Goods ordered from them;

(iii) Stock in warehouse;

(iv) Stock in shop;

(v) Stock level;

(vi) Order; (vii)Time lag between deliveries. See exhibit 12.01

BRANCH			COMPANY		REPRESENTATIVE		TEL.			DEPOT TEL. No.				

PRODUCT	SIZE	PRICE	PRICE CHANGES		STOCK LEVEL	Week No.		Week No.		Week No.		Week No.		Week No.		Week No.	
						S	O	S	O	S	O	S	O	S	O	S	O

Exhibit 12.01
Stock and Order Card

If these details are completed prior to the representative visiting the store, the manager will have an up-to-date picture of the total stock position.

(f) *Minimum stock level*

These figures are obviously used by most organisations as a guide to ordering. The average sales figure is important. This is the amount of stock required to ensure the store does not run out before the arrival of the next delivery. There are times when average figures need over-riding e.g. soft drinks in summer. It is also impossible to have stock levels for new lines. In both cases the experience and skill of the buyer is required.

2.6 *Security*

(a) Security of goods is essential and relies upon the honesty of staff, drivers, representatives, and merchandisers. All these people are a security risk. High risk goods e.g. wines, spirits, cigarettes and jewellery should be kept locked up in either special rooms or caged areas in the warehouse. The public should never be allowed in these places. Do not allow staff to wander around unnecessarily. It is sound policy not to allow junior or new members of staff to be in alone. Send them in with a more permanent or senior member. When the store is closed an effective alarm system should be used to detect intruders.

(b) Fire is a serious risk in any business and can destroy large quantities of stock. Businesses have been bankrupted by fire. Any goods which are a fire risk should be isolated from the rest of the stock. If possible these should be in fire proof rooms with a special alarm and extinguishing system. Examples would include paraffin, white spirit, paint, polystyrene or butane gas. It is now a legal requirement that every store room should have an adequate number of extinguishers plus adequate escape exits, both clearly marked and easily accessible. See also 9.6

12.7 *Exercise 2*

1. Design a layout for a stock control card. Apply this to goods with which you are familiar.

2. Explain the need for stock level figures.

3. What precautions would you take when storing high risk goods in warehouses.

12.8 **Assignments**

1. Critically appraise the method of receiving goods into your own store. Suggest ways of improving the system. Use the information gained in 12.4 Question 1 during the group discussion.

2. Investigate the stock control methods used in your own store. Suggest any improvements which could be made.

Chapter 13

Shop Stock

At the end of this chapter you should be able to:-

(A) Give examples of price marking and presentation of information on tickets.

(B) Explain the importance of effective stock keeping in the shop.

(C) Explain the need for security of goods in stock.

(D) Explain the need for commodity and merchandise knowledge.

(E) Describe the methods of obtaining commodity and merchandise knowledge.

In Chapter 12 we discussed how goods were received and stored ready for use on the shop floor. We will now examine some of the problems associated with stock, from its leaving the warehouse to the customer receiving it.

13.1 *Price tickets and price marking*

Pricing is a very important task. Legible tickets are a great help in selling. A clear distinguishable ticket is required i.e. one that can be readily identified by both staff and customer. Most organisations fix the prices at which their merchandise must be sold. It is the responsibility of the assistant to ensure the correct marking of the goods. Tickets can contain a great deal of information to assist stock taking and stock control methods. This information must be accurate and great care must be taken especially where written tickets are used.

(a) *Information on price tickets*

   (i) Price. This is essential for both customers and assistant. Price is often an important factor when deciding whether or not to purchase an article. It allows customers to compare prices between shops before purchasing.

   (ii) Description. Fashion shops need to put more information on their tickets to assist the customer. This will include size, material and possibly colour.

   (iii) Order Reference Number. This is important when re-ordering fresh stock. The reference number can be quoted to the buying department who will trace the supplier in their files. It also helps when dealing with complaints, to be able quickly to trace manufacturer or supplier.

(iv) Cost Price. This information is very important for stock checks, and at stock taking when goods are valued at cost price. It can also be used to assess price reductions during sales. All establishments record this information in code so as not to confuse the customer. These codes are common to a particular organisation and usually take the form of letters substituting for numbers. Cost price information should not be divulged to the customer. They are usually unaware of the expenses involved in running a retail shop.

(v) Department Code. This can be in the form of either letters or numbers and help to trace the exact location of the goods.

(vi) Date Code. This is the date the goods were received into the store, not necessarily the date they were put on the shelves. Many large stores use an open coding system e.g. 8/84 could stand for August 1984. Some organisations use different coloured tickets which are changed every six months. It is easy to spot old stock without checking the date. Coding aids stock rotation and readily identifies 'slow sellers'. Coloured tickets can also be used to segregate items e.g. sale goods or those on special offer. By reducing the time during which goods are displayed and handled, damage and soilage can be reduced to a minimum.

(b) *Methods of price marking* (See exhibit 13.01)

These vary between organisations and include some of the following:-

(i) By hand using a rubber stamp or felt tipped pen.

(ii) Printed adhesive labels which are dispensed from a machine or hand operated gun. These can be difficult to remove without leaving a mark. They are of limited use.

Both (i) and (ii) are used extensively in supermarkets or on items where no damage will occur to the merchandise.

(iii) Clip on tickets which clip on to woollen garments or skirts by means of a small wire clip at the top. Most of these are hand written. Their main disadvantage is that they can spoil the goods if they are incorrectly attached or removed. Another disadvantage is the creation of rust stains on the goods if the wire clips become wet.

(iv) Tie on tickets which vary in size are used extensively for hardware and fashion. These do not damage the goods but take time to fasten on. As they are larger in size than clip on tickets, they can contain a great deal of information.

(v) Plastic tie on tickets which are attached by means of a special gun. These are also used in fashion. The gun ejects the tie at speed and forces it through the material without damage. They cannot be pulled out without causing damage, and must be cut off.

83

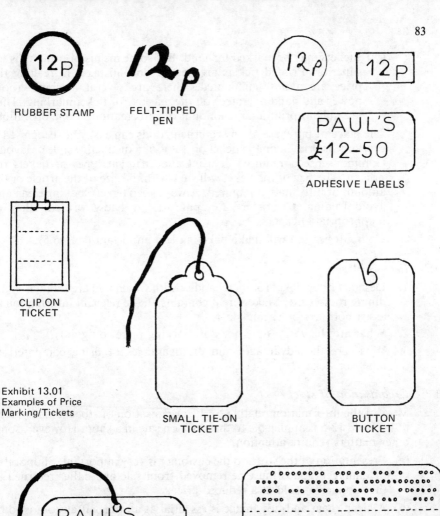

RUBBER STAMP

FELT-TIPPED PEN

ADHESIVE LABELS

PAUL'S
£12-50

CLIP ON TICKET

Exhibit 13.01
Examples of Price
Marking/Tickets

SMALL TIE-ON TICKET

BUTTON TICKET

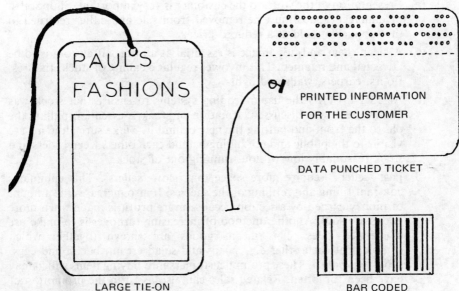

PAUL'S FASHIONS

PRINTED INFORMATION FOR THE CUSTOMER

DATA PUNCHED TICKET

LARGE TIE-ON TICKET

BAR CODED TICKET

(vi) Tickets may be marked by hand. But some means of printing is far superior. Printed tickets are neater, and mistakes in reading the price are almost eliminated. There are several machines (both power and hand operated) on the market for ticket marking. They are able to print a large amount of information in one operation.

The place of purchase of any returned goods can easily be recognised if the name is printed on the ticket or if it is of a distinctive style or layout. Commonsense is required in using the different types of tickets for pricing. The size of the ticket will vary with the size of the article or the amount of information required. Always keep tickets looking clean and avoid folding. Customers are 'put off' by badly written, dirty or inappropriate tickets.

Computerisation will make ticketing less important (see 16.5).

13.2   *Exercise 1*

1.   Design a price ticket for merchandise with which you are familiar e.g. a dining room suite. Make sure it contains all the relevant information to assist both customer and staff.
2.   What are the various methods of marking prices on goods?
3.   What are the advantages and disadvantages of using computerised labels or tickets?

13.3   *Organisation of stock*

Most of the information relating to the organisation of stock already given in 12.3 and 12.5 is applicable to the stock on sale in a shop. However, some other matters require attention.

(a)   Presentation of the stock to the customer is very important. Shop soiled or damaged goods must be removed from sale and either returned to the supplier or sold at a reduced price.

(b)   A clean, neat and tidy image is essential at all times if custom is to be attracted and retained. This involves regular cleaning of stock, fixtures, floors, carpets, walls and lights.

(c)   At 13.1 (a) (vi) the use of coding systems to ensure that stock was always fresh was discussed. Rotation of stock is essential, pulling the old to the front and putting the new behind it. Make sure all items are visible to the public and not hiding behind each other. Keep orders and stock reasonably low without running out of stock.

(d)   Fast 'sellers' require more space than slow 'sellers'. This eliminates constant filling and refilling of the shelves. It also increases the amount of money earned by a section because more profit is made when more goods are sold. Another method of increasing turnover is to make use of related sales. This means goods are shown together which complement each other e.g. salads and salad cream, bacon and eggs, shoes and polish. These prompt customers into buying items which may have been forgotten. Related sales can also assist in the promotion of slow selling lines.

(e) Care of stock is very important. As already mentioned in 13.1(a) (vi) damage can be reduced by reducing the amount of time the goods are on display. All stock can be damaged by careless handling from both customers and staff.

(i) Broken or cracked bottles can leak over the remainder of the stock e.g. broken squash bottles make the remainder sticky and destroy labels.

(ii) Bad fruit and vegetables will contaminate others in the pile and cause a smell.

(iii) Dust will quickly soil fashion goods especially those made of pastel coloured materials.

(iv) Water from leaking roofs or from the wet coats and hands of customers will mark or stain fabrics and wood, or destroy birthday and greeting cards.

(v) Broken fingernails will pull many materials, especially nylon.

(vi) Cigarettes will burn holes in plastics and man made fibres.

(f) Wherever possible try to organise an area where 'marked down' or damaged goods can be displayed. It will attract customers who are looking for a bargain and are not particular about a small defect. Specify that these items are not returnable, and that refunds will not be given. It will be the responsibility of the customer to ensure the goods are worth the price, or can be adapted to another use.

13.4 *Security of stock*

The security of warehouse stock has already been mentioned in 12.6. Shop stock is at a greater risk from thieves who intend to steal, and from careless customers and staff who break or damage the goods. See also 17.4 on display. Stock losses in any form reduce the profitability of an organisation. This in turn reduces the amount of money available to spend on improvements or expansion. Stock losses lead to leakage which is a term used to describe the difference between the planned sales value of purchases and the actual sales income. Many managers are assessed on their leakage figure. Good ones return a low figure, whilst poor ones return a high figure. Some organisations run an incentive scheme and pay a bonus each year for managers producing high turnover figures linked with a low leakage figure. See also 8.7b.

Some leakage is unavoidable e.g. price reductions on shop soiled items or weighing up losses (overweight). Losses can be classified into two areas:-

(a) Known losses, already mentioned, e.g. price reductions, discount, goods which have been written off.

(b) Unknown losses e.g. undercharging, overweighing, giving too much change, faulty checking (see 12.1) stealing or breakages.

As stealing makes up the major part of leakage, special care must be taken at all times to overcome it. Staff must always be vigilant and on the look out for customers who are acting strangely, or situations likely to help the thief.

Improvements to the layout of the shop can be made to:-

(a) eliminate blind spots;

(b) create uninterrupted views between aisles or stands;

(c) keep displays low to enable staff to see over them from any part of the shop;

(d) improve the lighting especially in dark corners;

(e) improve the presentation of the stock;

(f) incorporate the use of anti-theft devices such as mirrors; closed circuit television (CCTV), one way glass and the employment of specialist security organisations.

13.5   Merchandise knowledge

Merchandise knowledge is important to the sales assistant. It creates a good image and will produce satisfied customers. See also 14.4. Assistants should be aware of the stock in their department especially as to quantities, types, styles and range. It helps to know how many units of a particular range are available in the shop and where they are situated. In addition, the assistant must know how much and where goods of different kinds are in the stock room.

Information about deliveries is also of great use. If an assistant knows the time lag between deliveries, a more accurate picture can be built concerning new arrivals. This improves customer relations by reducing frustrating trips to the store whilst waiting for goods to arrive.

Merchandise knowledge can be gained from:-

(a) *The goods themselves.* Food items have labels, on which are listed ingredients, preparation instructions, and serving suggestions. Electrical and mechanical goods contain instructions which can be read. This is very important where demonstrations have to be given. Familiarisation is easier during quiet periods or when the shop is closed. Many sales are lost by assistants not knowing how the goods work or how to overcome problems.

(b) *Representatives.* Discussions with representatives can provide a useful source of information. They have first hand knowledge of their goods and market trends. Most manufacturers produce sales literature and technical data. Do not be too technical when talking to customers. Keep the language simple and easy to understand by the layman.

(c) *Trade Press.* Advertisements and articles appear regularly in the trade press which should be available for all the staff to read.

These magazines also contain a great deal of useful information concerning products, new lines, improved methods, future sales promotions, effective layouts and legislation affecting the shop and its products. They also contain articles giving advice and up-to-date price lists.

(d) *Trade Fairs and Exhibitions.* See also 17.7(g).

(e) *Visits to the factories of manufacturers.*

(f) *Libraries.* Most libraries contain a wealth of information. They are usually divided into reference and lending sections. The reference section will not lend out books, but information can be extracted from them. The information is normally kept up to date. It usually consists of:-

(i) Statistics on buying habits, market trends, and buying power of the public;

(ii) Companies and their products (KOMPASS);

(iii) Copies of magazines published by the Consumer Association (WHICH);

(iv) Acts of Parliament and new legislation;

(v) Methods and areas of production;

(vi) Patents on new and existing inventions;

(vii) Past issues of all the major magazines and newspapers.

Library lending sections allow books to be taken home for a period of up to three weeks. Ensure that any publication you use is up to date as facts and methods change. This is particularly important when looking up points of law.

Every town and college has a library. Make sure you know where it is and how to use it. If in doubt ask for assistance.

The knowledge an assistant will normally seek will depend on the goods his shop sells. It will include sources of supply, construction, maintenance, brands, alternative varieties or models, and particular features which require emphasis. This knowledge will help with enquiries and direct the customer to the best product available for the job within an acceptable price range.

13.6 Exercise 2

1. Imagine you are the manager of a large supermarket which has a large quantity of out of date cakes. Describe how you would deal with the situation from the point of view of:-

   a. clearing the stock

   b. ensuring that it does not occur again.

2. What are 'related sales' and why are they important?

3. Describe leakage. Give an example to show you understand its meaning. Why does leakage occur?

4. List the ways in which shop layout can be improved to reduce stealing.

13.7 Assignments

1. List and describe the methods used for pricing goods in your store. Give examples of the types of goods to which each method applies.

2. Taking an article of your own choice, list all the selling points which could be used in answer to a customer enquiry.

Chapter 14

Employers' Expectations

At the end of this chapter you should be able to:-
(A) Describe the likely expectations of an employer in relation to his staff.
(B) Explain the need for workplace cooperation.
(C) Recognise the nature and type of work undertaken.
(D) Appreciate the need to understand and carry out instructions.

4.1   *Does this apply to me?*

The points made in this chapter are relevant both to those in employment and those currently seeking it.

Those in employment will need at least to meet an acceptable minimum standard in order to retain their jobs and to do rather better if in future they hope for advancement. Those seeking employment will need to satisfy employers on this and other points, in order to obtain employment.

Potential employees have the opportunity in letters or application forms, and at the interview, to try to put across their suitability in terms of meeting employers' expectations, existing employees can demonstrate this in their workplace.

4.2   *General Expectations*

What then do most employers expect? Whilst no definitive standards can be laid down, it will obviously depend on the circumstances. Some employers have higher standards than others; standards will vary with the nature of the job, and also will change over time in response to what is thought acceptable by society.

These expectations may be examined under a number of headings i.e. loyalty, commitment, consistant work, honesty, good timekeeping, acceptable appearance and level of education.

The importance of each will to some extent be linked to the nature of the job. For a warehouseman away from contact with customers, appearance, provided the individual is clean, is of little importance, whilst in the case of a salesperson, appearance is extremely important.

These expectations can be explicit, that is, you are told what is expected or it is written into your contract of employment; or implicit, that is, you are not told in so many words but, by other means, you can see what is expected e.g. from your colleagues' behaviour. A shopkeeper may not have expressed as an expectation that his sales staff should be courteous and helpful to customers, most staff would automatically, on a commonsense basis, assume this to be the case.

14.3 *Loyalty*

This can take many forms and be expressed in various degrees of enthusiasm. Few British employers would expect or indeed welcome the singing of the company song around the company flag as occurs in some Japanese organisations.

What most employers require would be refraining from actions likely to damage the organisation such as:

(a) disparaging its goods or services to potential customers,

(b) 'leaking' information to others such as the passing on of trade secrets or commercial information to competitors,

(c) leaving and canvassing the business customers for your new employer or your own business,

(d) in certain circumstances setting up in competition against your ex-employer.

It is difficult to measure loyalty or the lack of it, a particularly sensitive employer may see mild criticism as the worst betrayal, and others may consider his staff joining a trade union as a form of disloyalty.

Serious cases of disloyalty often result in dismissal or some lesser punishment. In addition, the law protects the employer from some forms of disloyalty, for example, from an employee who having possibly received the benefit of a training with an organisation, sets up nearby in competition with it.

In general the courts take a reasonably balanced view in protecting the employer from the 'disloyal' acts of staff. An ex-employee setting up in competition with his former employer will only be restrained from doing so if the employee had:

(a) received substantial training or useful commercial knowledge,

(b) set up in competition within a reasonable time of leaving or reasonably close by,

(c) posed a realistic threat to his former employer.

The ex employee of a large grocery store who left and returned a couple of years later, setting up a small shop in a distant part of the same large town, would not be restrained by the courts. They have to balance the need to encourage competition against the need to protect existing businesses from past employees who, because of these former links with it, may have some slight advantages.

Divided loyalties – many organisations prohibit their employees from engaging in activities which might create a conflict of loyalties e.g. retailers prohibiting their staff from private trading.

Divided loyalties can also be a problem when loyalty is owed to more than one cause and situations arise when the loyalty owed to one is in conflict with that owed to another e.g. loyalty to your friends v loyalty to your employer.

In such cases only you can decide where your loyalty lies in a given situation, to minimise such potential conflicts organisations often take pains to put certain people into certain types of job.

4.4 Commitment

This is often taken to mean how hard and enthusiastically people work or play. Football commentators have used the word to describe certain players. Often commitment is linked to loyalty.

The degree of commitment shown by an employee is most obviously reflected in the standard and quantity of his work. Most employers have rules and procedures for dealing with those whose work is not up to standard.

How else can commitment be assessed? The following would suggest commitment:

(a) working voluntary overtime at very short notice,

(b) staying behind or working over a lunch break in order to ensure a job is completed on time,

(c) taking work home,

(d) taking trouble to obtain as wide a product knowledge as possible,

(e) furthering education in order to make oneself into a better qualified and more useful employee,

(f) getting to work in appalling weather conditions, especially if no transport is available.

Employers looking for evidence of commitment in potential employees might consider:

(a) the care and thought put into the letter or form of application,

(b) some indication to find out about the area, organisation and job plus interest in the job and possible promotion prospect,

(c) interest in training,

(d) evidence of commitment in other areas e.g. in sporting activities,

(e) academic progress.

What employers do not like to see is indications of drifting aimlessly as illustrated by having had several jobs over a very short period unless circumstances, i.e. family of health reasons, made such moves necessary. This indicates a lack of commitment.

Most employers are realistic in terms of the level of commitment they expect given the extent of other commitments most people have. Some people are 'married' to their job and give it priority over all other commitments. Such people tend to be in relatively senior positions and often pay a high price in terms of social and family pleasures foregone.

14.5 *Consistent work*

This involves working at a constant standard usually at a level of competence and output that is acceptable. In a shop this may be taken to include a lack of, or small number of mistakes in pricing goods, shelves always stocked, floors clean and rubbish cleared away.

Most employers if they had to make a choice between someone who gets on and does the job reliably at a steady if unspectacular pace and one who is somewhat erratic who will perform spectacularly well one day and abysmally the next, will opt for the former who exhibits consistency – they know where they stand with him and can plan accordingly. This is especially true in relation to routine though nonetheless important tasks of which there are many in distribution.

14.6 *Good timekeeping*

Those of you who have stood in the pouring rain or bitter cold waiting for a friend who turns up late will appreciate the importance of good timekeeping if only for a limited time. Employers appreciate its importance on a much more permanent basis, time really is money to them.

Poor timekeeping by staff means they are paying for a commodity they are not receiving – your time. It may result in:

(a) late opening and loss of potential custom,

(b) additional losses from pilfering due to inadequate staff cover,

(c) build up of queues of customers causing ill feeling and potential loss of custom.

Many organisations require their employees to "clock on" as this provides a fairly reliable measure of timekeeping. In smaller distributive organisations, employing few staff, this is usually unnecessary.

Very few of us are never late so the occasional lapse is acceptable and made more so by phoning in to explain the position. If you are to be more than a few minutes late, then other arrangements can then be made.

It is certainly in your interest to be a good timekeeper since:

(a) sanctions such as reprimands, loss of pay and possibly eventual dismissal can result,

(b) it effects your colleagues who may have to work harder or forego part of their break to cover for you, which will not endear you to them.

Absences – most distributive trades organisations operate on very tight staff budgets and so carry little spare capacity in terms of extra staff so absences, especially of a prolonged nature, can cause great difficulty.

Most absences are unavoidable e.g. through illness, and employers recognise this. However, absenteeism for frivolous reasons is likely to be viewed dimly. Absences are recorded for National Insurance and other purposes e.g. for accident reports.

4.7 *Exercise 1*
1. Define divided loyalties.
2. How might an interview aid an employer in assessing suitability?
3. Why are employers keen on good timekeeping?
4. Suggest reason why prolonged or unexpected absence from work can cause problems.

4.8 *Acceptable appearance*

Appearance not only covers dress but also grooming, deportment and cleanliness.

In distribution you must not only meet a standard acceptable to your employers, but also other more or less stringent standards set by customers if you wish to gain their confidence and hence their custom.

You must also comply with certain laws which lay down standards which have a bearing on appearance e.g. Health and Safety at Work Act and the Food Hygiene regulations.

4.9 *Honesty*

Many wholesale and retail outlets have large amounts of cash and valuable stock on the premises, so the need for honesty is self-evident. Various surveys on theft from distributors indicate that considerable losses occur through staff failings in this area.

Many distributors' standards in this respect are absolute, they will discipline, often by dismissal, anyone found to be dishonest, even though the amount involved is relatively small.

Since, in most cases, others have the opportunity to steal e.g. deliverymen and customers, because of this and other reasons, the employer cannot use the 'shrinkage' figure as an indication of staff honesty.

4.10 *Employers' obligations*

The discussion so far may give you the impression that the employer is asking for a lot but what might you ask is he offering in exchange?

Many of the more obvious items, such as pay and holidays, are set out in the contract on employment. However, in addition to these many employers provide

(a) bonus schemes,
(b) staff discount facilities,
(c) subsidised canteen meals,
(d) other welfare facilities,

to encourage employees to identify with the business and show them that they regard them as valuable members of the organisation.

Such tangible expressions of concern for staff wellbeing usually bring rich rewards in terms of loyalty etc. Many of the most successful distribution concerns make generous provisions in this area – a policy of enlightened self interest.

14.11 *Co-operation with colleagues*

The vast majority of us get on with and co-operate with our colleagues. It is in everyones interest that this occurs for both social and business reasons.

(a) Social –
  (i) we spend a large part of our time at work, too long to spend at loggerheads with each other.
  (ii) just as school and college provides us with a circle of friends so work provides further opportunities for friendship and possible marriage.

(b) Business –
  (i) generally speaking the more we cooperate the easier it is to get things done.
  (ii) lack of co-operation can cause delay, out of stock situations etc., which create a bad image for the business and can result in loss of trade.

14.12 *Carrying out instructions*

Many students reading this will have little experience of distribution work so will need to pay particular attention to what is said. You will not be in a position to argue about the merits of instructions given.

However, this does not mean that you should unthinkingly carry out instructions about which you feel unhappy. Ask, most employers and other experienced staff are usually willing to explain both the reasons for the instructions and how they should be carried out. Remember that often it is only by asking that you can increase your knowledge of the business, its products and the way it does things. Another reason for asking is to obtain clarification of your instructions, better to ask and make sure rather than have a go. The results of not understanding can have safety, legal or financial implications for yourself and your employer.

14.13 *Adaptability*

Whilst most jobs in distribution especially those at a junior level involve a large amount of routine repetitive work such as shelf filling, pricing and till operation, there is a need for you to be adaptable.

This arises in a number of situations:

(a) In order to increase staff flexibility to ensure, for example, that if a cashier is missing another member of staff can replace her. Seasonal factors and holidays may also call for a flexible response.

(b) Promotion in distribution is based largely on experience, which includes experience in all or most facets of the operation of a retail outlet or warehouse.

Adaptability is desirable in a more general sense in that it is most unlikely that you will be able to spend your working life doing the same job.

Distribution though still offers to the bulk of new entrants a chance to deal with people on a personal basis and given the diversity (some would say perversity) of the public it need never be uninteresting.

14.14 *Exercise 2*

1. Name three jobs in distribution where appearance is important and three where it is not.
2. Why do employers demand high standards of honesty?
3. Suggest why employers are likely to provide overalls to many employees.
4. Other than those mentioned in the text, give two examples of routine tasks likely to occur in distribution.
5. Why may holidays call for more staff flexibility?

14.15 **Assignments**

1. Briefly describe and place in order of importance the various employers expectations discussed in this chapter from the point of view of a high class jeweller wishing to recruit a young trainee salesperson. Give reasons for the order chosen.
2. Imagine you are a manager composing a reference for someone who has worked in your organisation for several years and has applied for a better job elsewhere. Write the reference illustrating how this young person has met your expectations.

Chapter 15

The Selling Function

At the end of this chapter you should be able to:-
(A) Identify the various selling methods.
(B) Explain the need to establish appropriate personal standards.
(C) Demonstrate the ability to deal with differing sales situations.
(D) List and describe the methods of payment used in retail outlets.
(E) List the stages involved when handling cash and verifying cheques and credit notes.
(F) Describe the forms of credit used in retail outlets.
(G) Describe the procedure for sales on credit.
(H) Explain how complaints can arise and how to handle them.
(I) Explain how to deal with exchanges, refunds and credit notes.

15.1 *Selling methods*

There are three basic selling methods used in retailing:-
(a) Counter or personal service
(b) Self-selection
(c) Self-service

Each method has its own way of satisfying customer needs.

(a) *Counter Service*

This has been established for a long time. It was the first method used by retailers. The customer is given personal service by the assistant who helps with the choice of goods. Customers normally accept the recommendations or advice of the salesman. Usually this promotes goodwill between them. In turn this goodwill assists in promoting the reputation of the store. It is of great value in image building and promotion of sales. (See also Chapters 17 and 18).

The assistant determines the exact needs of the customer by asking questions about, for example, type, colour and size of the merchandise required. He will also need to know whether the intended purchase is for personal use or for a gift. It is also necessary to find out how much the customer is prepared to spend. Many customers have only a vague idea of what they need. In such cases advice is always required so that the customers' exact needs are satisfied.

Personal service is essential where small expensive items are involved e.g. jewellery. It is also used where goods require expert technical advice e.g. expensive hi-fi equipment. A large number of staff are required for this method to be successful. The goods in shops using this method tend to be more expensive than in those where it is not employed.

(b) *Self Selection*

Self selection allows the customer to browse around the merchandise without being pestered by sales staff. If advice is required then staff are available to help. One of the problems is knowing the extact time to approach a customer during the browsing period. If an assistant approaches too soon customers may feel they are being forced into a sale. When the approach is too late, both the customer and the sale are lost. A customer who spends a great deal of time looking at an article is often requiring assistance. In addition one who is speedily searching the shelves may also be requiring assistance. An approach of "Can I help you" or "Is there anything I can show you" will usually prompt a negative reply, e.g. "No, I am only looking". This ends the conversation and leaves the assistant with no other avenue of approach. Do not ask questions which can be answered by "Yes" or "No". Involve the customer in conversation. Try to obtain more information about the goods in which she appears to be interested. Use your product knowledge (see also 13.5) to approach the customer.

For example:-

(i) "This is a new line".

(ii) "We have that range in various colours".

(iii) "Customers have recommended this to their friends".

(iv) "We use it at home and find it very useful".

The customer will usually give more information about her shopping needs. The assistant is then in a better position to help meet them.

Self selection uses the open counter presentation adopted by Marks and Spencers, British Home Stores and other large stores. Staff are employed in attending to the counter presentation. Others deal exclusively with receiving payments for goods sold. There are many "cash and wrap" areas spread throughout the store where the customer pays for the goods.

A further characteristic of self selection is the use of many exits and entrances through which the customers may leave or enter the store. In addition the customer should be allowed to pay for a purchase at any of the cash points and continue to browse around the displays.

(c) *Self Service*

In 5.9 we examined the growth of the supermarket due to the shortage of staff and the need for increasing the speed at which customers can shop. Full self service has been developed where the customer selects and collects the goods and pays for them at the checkout. The basic difference between self selection and self service is the way by which payment is made. In self selection the customer can pay for the goods at any cash point in the store during the shopping expedition. By contrast, in self service stores, the customer pays for the goods at the end of the shopping expedition just prior to leaving the store.

A different form of salesmanship is used in self service. It relies on attractive goods selling themselves through display, colour (see Chapter 18) and impulse buying. Stores are laid out so that the customer is guided round. Her attention is drawn to the maximum amount of goods on sale.

Self service situations need not be devoid of all service. Staff are employed to fill the shelves and keep the store tidy. If they are well trained they can also assist customers with a problem. The benefits of self service can then be combined with some of the advantages of personal service.

15.2 *The essentials of a sales assistant*

(a) *Appearance*

Sales staff should be clean, neat and tidy in both appearance and dress. Long hair should be tied back especially when handling food. It is essential to wear freshly laundered overalls. People who keep themselves looking neat and tidy do not enjoy working in untidy conditions. A clean and tidy shop with smart assistants creates a good public image for the store. See also 8.4(e).

(b) *Communication*

We shall see later that communications are essential to people in the retail trade. Sales assistants should be good, clear speakers, able to converse with all types of customers. Do not put on an act. Just be natural.

(c) *Personality*

Your personality will be projected to the customer who will react accordingly e.g. a smile will bring a smile. To be a good sales assistant you must have a liking for people and be pleasant and courteous at all times.

(d) *Product Knowledge*

We discussed in 13.5 the need for product knowledge and how it can assist the salesman. Show an interest in the goods you sell and bring out their selling points. If you are not interested in the goods on sale, why should the customer be interested?

(e) *Commonsense*

You will need a great deal of commonsense when dealing with the general public. Develop a mature outlook, especially when the customer is being 'childish'. Experience is the only way to learn how to handle different situations. No two are alike.

15.3 *Exercise 1*

1. Distinguish between self selection and self service.

2. What type of selling method would you use for:-

    (a) a toy shop in the centre of a large city.

    (b) a high class confectioners in a large housing estate.

3. Imagine you are the manager of a large store. What points would you look for in the ideal sales assistant?

15.4 *Customer Relations* (see also 10.1)

Customers are the most important people to enter your shop. Without customers a shop cannot survive. It must have a large number of regular satisfied customers.

Customers must have confidence in the staff and rely on their knowledge and expertise. It is essential therefore to build up this knowledge by taking an interest in the products you sell and in the company for which you work. (See also 13.5).

All people are different and require different treatment. Moods vary from day to day. They can change with the weather! The only way to be fairly certain of understanding a person is to have known him or her for many years. There is little time to get to know customers unless they are 'regulars'.

Treat the customer in the way you would like to be treated. Their dislikes are often your dislikes. Customers like a cheerful smile, politeness, pleasant personality, and to be treated as someone special. They do not like rudeness, curtness, indifference and being ignored. See also 15.2.

If you are feeling depressed, tired or under the weather, it will show in your manner, in your attitude or even on your face.

Never react angrily to an angry customer. Try to calm down those who are irate. Take the heat out of the situation. "Cool it" is a popular phrase nowadays. It is certainly one a good sales assistant should remember.

15.5 *Methods of payment*

(a) *Cash*

Payment by cash is the most popular method used in a shop to settle transactions. There is a limit to the quantity of money in the form of coins that can be given to pay for goods. This is known as legal tender. See also 1.5

There are rules governing the handling of cash which must be followed in order to avoid errors.

(i) Place the customer's money on the ledge of the till. If a note has been tendered, put it in the clip provided on the front of the till. Never put money in the till until the change has been given. This will stop any arguments from customers concerning incorrect change.

(ii) Count the change out of the till unless it is one which calculates change.

(iii) Count the change into the customer's hand.

(iv) Place the customer's money in the till and close the drawer. Never leave a till drawer open or be away from an unlocked till.

(v) Always take the money and give the change before the goods are wrapped.

Most organisations have rules to follow if an error is made in ringing up the amount. This may involve cancelling the previous receipt and issuing a new one. It should not involve adjusting the price of goods taken from another customer. In all cases, a card or document will have to be filled in with details of the error and signed by a senior member of staff. This helps the cashier to balance the till by adjusting any errors. If you have no authority to alter amounts, you must always seek assistance from a supervisor or manager. See exhibit 15.01.

OVER-RING CARD		
TILL No.		**DATE**
AMOUNT		AUTHORISED BY

Exhibit 15.01
Over-ring Card

When handling large amounts of cash a till routine must be adopted and followed, by all members of staff. Ensure there is an adequate 'float' (enough change and notes to start with) and change provided for the tills in use. Do not allow large amounts to accumulate, especially at peak periods. Remove notes at periodic intervals. When moving large sums of money between the tills and cash office, take special security precautions. At least two persons should do this job.

(b) *Cheques*

Payment by cheque is becoming popular as it does not involve the customer in carrying large amounts of cash. Although the procedure for accepting cheques is simple, it must be followed carefully. Cheque books can be lost or stolen and the finder or thief is able to buy goods. In such cases the firm accepting the cheques will not be paid by the bank.

If a customer wishes to pay by cheque, only accept a Banker's Card or Cheque Card as proof of identity. Ensure the following details are accurately checked:-

(i) Signature on cheque card corresponds with that of the cheque;

(ii) The card has not expired;

(iii) The card number is entered on the reverse of the cheque;

(iv) The date is correct;

(v) The cheque is correctly made payable to the shop;

(vi) The words and figures agree;

(vii) The bank code number on the card agrees with that on the cheque (except in the case of Barclaycards which can be used as cheque cards);

(viii) Any alterations have been initialled.

Some companies only allow senior members of staff to check these details and approve a cheque. If this is your company's policy carry it out. Cheque cards will allow the customer to purchase up to £50 of goods in one transaction. The bank guarantees payment if the correct procedure has been adopted. Many supermarkets allow customers to cash cheques at a cash point before shopping. This eliminates the checkout operator handling cheques and increases the flow of customersthrough the checkouts.

See exhibit 15.02

Is the date correct
↓

← Is this the code on the card

← Is the name correct

← Do the words and numbers agree

← Does this look like the signature on the card

← Is the card current

↗
Is this the code on the cheque

↑
This must be written on the back of the cheque

Exhibit 15.02
Transacting a Cheque

(c) *Credit Cards*

The two most commonly used are Access and Barclaycard but some retailers have their own "in house" cards. Again adopt the correct procedure laid down for accepting credit cards.

(i) Check the card has not expired;

(ii) Fill in the details on the payment slips e.g. date, goods, amount, total;

(iii) Place the customer's credit card in the space provided on the machine;

(iv) Place the completed slips in the correct position;

(v) Draw the handle smartly forward and back over the payment slips. Details of the store and customer card will now be printed on the payment slips.

(vi) Ask the customer to sign the slips;

(vii) Check that the details appear on all the copies by looking at the bottom copy. It is sometimes necessary to press on hard, especially when the customer is signing.

(viii) Check the signature on the card agrees with that on the payment slips.

(ix) Give the top copy to the customer and place the remainder in the till.

Note that transactions of over £50 require to be verified by contacting Barclaycard or Access.

5.6 *Credit*

Credit trading enables a customer to buy goods without having to provide cash immediately. Once the goods have been handed over, the method by which they are paid for depends on the type of credit being allowed. The use of credit cards (which many organisations accept as being as near a cash transaction as possible) we have already examined. See 15.5(c)

Other forms of credit affect the store by 'tying up' money which is owed by the customers. In other words the retailer is unable to use money which he has loaned to customers until they pay it back.

(a) *Simple Credit*

This is allowed by the corner shop when a customer buys goods and pays for them at the end of the week.

(b) *Personal (monthly) Accounts*

Customers are allowed to buy goods from the shop up to an agreed amount. No deposit is made and the goods are paid for at the end of the month. A statement is sent to the customer itemising all purchases and allowing a short period of time for payment.

(c) *Budget Accounts*

In this case customers regularly pay a fixed amount per month into their account with the store. They may then buy on credit goods worth several times the amount paid. Interest is charged on any outstanding balance.

(d) *Hire Purchase*

Business is usually transacted by a retailer with the aid of a Finance Company (the owner of the goods). The 'hirer' is the customer i.e. the person taking possession of the goods and having use of them. The 'owner' is the Finance Company who hire the goods to the hirer and receives payment. In all cases the hirer can only take possession of the goods after paying the appropriate deposit. Repayments are made by instalments over an agreed period of time. The goods do not belong to the hirer until all payments have been made. Companies include an 'Option to Purchase' clause in the agreement. This involves the hirer paying a fixed sum e.g. £5 when the account is cleared, as a token payment for the transfer of goods. Interest is charged on the total sum borrowed and calculated over the agreement period.

Hire Purchase agreements are controlled by law. If payments are not made regularly, or the customer stops paying altogether, then the company can repossess the goods. This requires a court order if more than one third of the agreement price has been paid.

(e) *Credit Sale*

It is important to distinguish between hire purchase and a credit sale. In hire purchase the goods do not become the property of the customer until the last instalment has been paid and the option to purchase exercised. In credit sales the goods become the property of the customer from the first payment. They cannot be repossessed if the buyer defaults but money outstanding can be recovered in court. Interest is charged on the transaction.

Some retail outlets offer interest free credit to attract custom. Customers requiring credit facilities are investigated before being allowed to enter into an agreement. Any store has the right to refuse credit. It is not the automatic right of every customer.

15.7 *Exercise 2*

1. A customer arrives at your counter with a box of wine glasses valued at £4.36. She offers you a £10 note to pay for the glasses. Explain in logical sequence the steps involved in serving the customer.

2. Describe the points which require checking when accepting a cheque.

15.8 *Complaints*

(a) *Complaints from customers* — These usually fall into two categories:-

(i) Service;
(ii) Merchandise.

Most complaints are genuine, they should be treated as such until proved otherwise. Never be aggressive towards a customer even if they are aggressive towards you. Try to calm them down and obtain a clear picture of the complaint. There are always two 'sides' to a complaint. Beware of apologising before you know the facts. This gives the impression that the store is always wrong, which is not always the case.

Complaints of service are difficult to avoid in times of staff shortages when customers think they should be served immediately. A hard pressed assistant can quickly lose her temper. This merely adds to the customers annoyance. Assure the customer that the store is doing all it can under the circumstances. In these cases it is sound policy to seek further help from senior staff. Pass the complaint on to the section head or manager, who will have wider experience than an assistant in such matters.

Complaints concerning merchandise are very common, especially in mass produced goods. Minor defects tend to be overlooked by checkers and the majority of complaints are genuine. Assure the customer the fault will be rectified as soon as possible. Always replace faulty goods putting the returned goods on one side until they can be repaired or returned to the supplier. Check that the replacement is not faulty. Sometimes a whole delivery can have the same fault. If so, remove them all from sale. This applies especially to food which can have serious effects on customers (e.g. food poisoning). Such problems usually lead to publicity, causing drastic reductions in sales.

(b) *Overcoming Complaints*

The most successful way of overcoming complaints is to try not to let them happen.

(i) Do not invite complaints, especially when providing a service e.g. dry cleaning or hairdressing. Always ask positive questions. 'You don't think the colour is too dark for you?' can prompt a complaint from a customer who has had her hair colour rinsed.

(ii) Do not become involved in arguments this only irritates the customer and makes the situation worse. Never answer back or be rude. Always 'bite your tongue'. You will often find the customer is not always right. (e.g. if a customer complains about a woollen garment which has lost its shape, it may have been caused by not following the washing instructions and no fault of the shop).

You must prove this to him/her without being aggressive.

(iii) Make sure that you know your merchandise. See also 13.5. Point out to the customer any special instruction. e.g. never clean silver with an abrasive pad, no matter how tarnished it becomes.

(iv) Never make promises which cannot be kept such as firm promises regarding delivery dates or when ordering special purchases. Send the customer a card when the goods arrive.

(v) Do not ignore complaints by shrugging off those which do not apply to you. Help the customer by putting him in touch with the appropriate person.

(vi) Do not push complaints on one side and forget about them. This applies especially to written complaints. It only irritates a customer who may be waiting for an urgent reply. Prompt action will alleviate the situation.

(vii) Check all the goods as they arrive. Remove any that are faulty. Rotate stock to keep it fresh, and segregate any shop soiled item see 13.3(f)

(viii) Always keep the store clean. Many complaints arise from a dirty store. See 8.2(b)

15.9　*Customers Legal Rights*

When a store sells goods to a customer a contract is made between them. This means that it is up to the store to deal with unsatisfactory goods and not the manufacturer. All goods sold should comply with the 'Sale of Goods Act 1979': –

(a) The goods should be of merchantable quality.

This means that they should not be damaged or broken and must work correctly e.g. a table may have deep scratch on it or an automatic electric toaster may burn the toast.

(b) The goods must be as described.

This means the goods must correspond with the description on the label e.g. a can labelled 'plums' must not contain peas.

(c) The goods must be fit for the purpose for which they are intended. This means the purpose for which a customer will buy these particular goods.

A customer must specify if the intended purchase is for a special purpose.

If a shop sells faulty goods, it has broken its side of the contract. A customer can then cancel the purchase or ask for a refund on what has been paid. Most people ask for the goods to be replaced or repaired. Where there is any doubt with a purchase ask the customer to retain the receipt and return the goods if unsuitable e.g. buying a pair of shoes for someone else. Remember a customer cannot complain about faults which have already been pointed out to him by the shopkeeper. See also 13.3(f).

If a customer merely changes his mind about the purchase, he has no right to any compensation e.g. a customer buys a blue dress and wants to exchange it later for a red one. A case like this has to be treated on its merits. Many shops would make an exchange under these circumstances, as a boost to customer relations. Some customers take advantage of stores whose policy is to exchange goods whatever the reason.

15.10　*Credit Notes*

The practice of issuing credit notes for returned goods is gradually being discontinued by many businesses. Most customers know their rights and demand repayment. If a customer refuses a credit note for a genuine complaint, repay without question. This line of action enhances customer relations. Some customers will accept a credit note if a replacement is being delivered with new stock. Never ask a customer to purchase other goods to the value of those being returned. Remember that if customers accept a credit note for returned goods they have no direct right to their money back if at a later date they decide not to buy anything from the store.

15.11 *Exercise 3*

1. Briefly describe how you would deal with an irate customer returning a faulty transistor radio.
2. List the methods of overcoming complaints.
3. Name the conditions required by the 'Sale of Goods Act 1979'.

15.12 **Assignments**

1. Investigate the types of credit used in your own store. Explain how each type satisfies the needs of the customer.
2. Explain in detail the method your own store uses to deal with customer complaints.
3. Design a check list which can be used by an employer in selecting suitable employees.

Chapter 16

The Impact of New Technology on Distribution

At the end of this chapter you should be able to:-

(A) Identify the effects of modern computer-based systems on the distributive trade.

(B) Recognise the application of modern computer-based systems of
   (a) sales recording
   (b) stock recording
   (c) control and re-ordering
   (d) customer accounting
   (e) credit control.

16.1 *Introduction*

Initially there were four main considerations for developing computers in the distribution industry,

(a) administrative systems had become dated;

(b) there was a lack of adequate management information;

(c) the introduction of VAT;

(d) manual systems were unable to cope with the growing pressure of work.

The majority of hardware manufacturers have produced standard packages to suit different types of outlets but will produce tailor made systems according to the size and requirements of a store. Computers have made the greatest impact in:

(a) sales analysis
(b) purchasing
(c) budgeting
(d) wages systems
(e) personnel information systems
(f) shrinkage analysis
(g) staff performance
(h) cost/sell price structure
(j) master product files
(k) order preparation
(l) warehouse systems
(m) accounting
(n) invoice comparison
(o) payment systems.

Although investment costs for computerised systems can be extremely high, they should be offset by a distinct improvement in labour productivity. The increased capability of computers has been accompanied by a rapid decrease in costs which gives firms an incentive to either install computers for the first time or to expand existing systems.

Basically there are three levels of hardware sophistication used in the industry, depending on individual requirements.

(a) Electronic cash registers, similar to electromagnetic cash registers.

(b) Stand alone data capture units, carrying out the normal functions of a cash register and also recording information on magnetic tape which can be removed and processed through the computer.

(c) Fully computerised laser scanning, controlled whether by an in-store mini-computer or an on-line computer connected with a telecommunications link (more flexible than (b)).

In looking at the impact of technological developments on the industry, it is important to examine not only current technical changes, but the changes within the industry itself.

6.2 Cashless society

The silicon chip has allowed computer networks to be produced cheaply enough to enable most outlets to perform electronic banking functions where bank accounts are automatically debited when a purchase is made (either in a computerised store or on a home computer terminal). This will have the effect of reducing cash, cheques and credit card transactions, although the use of cash will never completely disappear. We could become not only a cashless society but a paperless society, where bills are paid without the inconvenience of writing a cheque or paying cash. Businesses in general, and retailers especially, spend much of their time and money on handling and protecting their cash. The UK banking system is now highly computerised, the handling of money and the processing of cheques and other documents slows down their efficiency.

Remember, however, for a fully integrated cashless society, every person must have a bank account, and other financial institutions, such as the Post Office or Building Societies will have to be incorporated into the scheme.

6.3 Electronic fund transfer systems

Electronic fund transfer (EFT) systems require the linking of cash registers, on line, to a bank computer. The system permits the immediate transfer of funds between two or more parties, and allows banking transactions outside normal banking hours in more convenient locations. The siting of banks in large stores is not a new feature and banking services could be extended to include:

(a) direct debiting for cash withdrawals;

(b) direct debiting for purchases;

(c) the transfer of money from one account to another;

(d) arranging a debit for a bill or loan repayment.

A bank card is presented to the cashier who inserts it in the computerised till for reading and verification. For added security the customer keys in their own personal identity number before the electronic signal goes to the bank to debit the account. All transactions are automatically checked by the card holders' bank before money is transferred to the retailer's account. The French are already making extensive use of off line terminals in connection with their EFT at the point-of-sale. Retailers use low cost off line credit authorisation terminals which store transaction details electronically on cartridge or disc which are sent to the card issuer for processing at a later date.

In 1980 NCR, in conjunction with the French Bank Credit Agricole instituted their first EFT system in three hypermarkets in Central France. Their intention is to extend the system to smaller retailers.

There is still much debate as to whether the existing system of cash, cheques and credit cards should be replaced. At the time of writing the EFT revolution has been slow to take off.

16.4 Exercise 1

1. What were the four main considerations for developing computers in the distribution industry?
2. Within the distribution industry where have computers made the greatest impact?
3. Why will we never become a cashless society?
4. Describe the Electronic Funds Transfer System.

16.5 Scanning

Article numbering was designed to improve efficiency throughout the distribution network identifying products by a system of numbers represented as machine readable bar code symbols. Scanning requires a bar code to be printed on the product to transfer product information onto a computer without the operator using a keyboard. Prices are marked on the shelves, not on the goods, and are recorded on the till receipt. Scanning is the most important modern development allowing the retailer to capture information on what has or has not been sold. Businesses which have incorporated scanning are becoming increasingly more efficient, improving their productivity and turnover.

Considerable data is generated by scanning which, when processed, will serve as a basis for company research into profitability, productivity and consumer trends. As retailers develop their scanning systems more pressure will be exerted on manufacturers to speed up their coding of labels.

0 20248 003885

Exhibit 16.01
Bar Code Label

6.6 Portable computer data recording terminals

The development of the microchip has reduced the size of terminals to that of a pocket calculator. It allows the retailer to prepare and place an order faster than the traditional price list/order form (PLOF) method or stock and order form using an ordinary telephone as the link to a central computer. For the system to function effectively, every item of merchandise must be assigned a code. This code is entered into the terminal, together with the quantity required, either in single units or in case lots depending on company policy. The product code is printed on a shelf edge label and the assistant makes an entry wherever stock is required. Wand scanners are now superseding the manual keying of data, speeding up the ordering process. Every entry is displayed on the keyboard for checking and any rogue entries are detected by the terminal.

Information is transmitted via a modem to a magnetic tape receiver housed in the distributor's computer centre (a process taking around 2-3 minutes). The tape is then fed through the computer in the normal way, and a picking list is printed.

6.7 Personal computers

Personal computers are most commonly thought of as consumer products, but now they are being developed for use by small retailers. In conjunction with portable data recording terminals they can be used as a packaged system which will read bar coded labels and carry out data processing on the information gathered.

6.8 Stocktaking

Traditional methods of stocktaking are very time consuming, labour intensive and expensive. It has been proved that actual sales drop whilst stocktaking is being carried out. When programmable hand held data capture terminals are used it simplifies the operation as assistants can be quickly trained to key in the information. Stocktakers have sole responsibility for keying information from product tags or tickets, with a supervisor only checking at regular intervals. Once the information has been satisfactorily entered it is processed, and any inaccuracies noticed are immediately checked. The need for extensive preparation is gone as in the traditional method, and stock can be recorded in any order. Stocktaking time is substantially reduced, it is no longer the headache it used to be, there is less disruption in the store, sales staff are free to help customers and stock takers are less obvious.

16.9 Stock control

In stock ordering systems, based on shelf edge labelling, the assistant counts the number of items on the shelf, and if less than the minimum stock level is displayed, the product requires ordering. The assistant keys in the product code and repeats the process throughout the store. Stock information is transmitted from the terminal to the computer via a telephone line.

Increased productivity is achieved by:

(a) reducing delivery lead times,

(b) increasing levels of direct shelf replenishment,

(c) reducing backroom stock.

When the order arrives at the store it is scanned and stock levels are updated by the computer, management being alerted of any stock shortages. As breakdowns in the system are fairly infrequent, this method of stock control can be relied on by both retailer and wholesaler.

Many distribution organisations are using computerised tills. Price tickets with data punched into them are fed through to produce a detailed printed receipt. At the same time the item is deducted from the total stock figure. Thus, it is possible to tell the stock position of any item at any time. From the information can be deduced the best selling lines, sizes, colours, styles and price ranges. These stock control methods do not preclude physical stock taking which is often done at regular intervals throughout the year. It is only then that any discrepancies are high-lighted by comparing the theoretical stock figure with the actual stock figure.

Essentially the computer is a stock control aid, from the data provided it will suggest future orders.

16.10 View data systems

Prestel is a good example of a computerised information service which can be used either in the home or business. The information is displayed on a special Prestel television receiver which is connected to the telephone via a modem. Each set has a small remote keyboard, about the size of a pocket calculator, through which the central computer is connected to the receiver. There is no need to lift the telephone receiver, Prestel announces itself by greeting the operator, personally, on the screen. The computer will then display an index of information available to the operator. Prestel information can be obtained on a wide range of subject areas such as income tax, holidays, travel, computer based games and electronic mail (a new development).

Prestel sets are more expensive than ordinary television sets, but beyond this initial outlay, the owner pays only for the service when in use (at the cost of a local telephone call) plus a small usage charge and the cost of the information displayed on the screen (this cost varies with the information required). The operator can also display a page which will outline the exact amount owing at any particular date.

There are similar view-data computerised information systems, using the ordinary household television as a VDU such as the teletext services of CEEFAX (BBC) and ORACLE (ITV). At present these systems have limited use, they utilise spare scanlines on the television screen to provide pages of information, but do not allow the operator to continue a dialogue, as in the Prestel system.

Tesco, Gateshead MBC and the University of Newcastle have developed a computer aided shopping services aimed at bringing the advantages of the superstore to those people who are either housebound or confined to shopping in a local area. The service is based in a branch library and uses modern POS equipment to enable customers to order goods for later delivery. In addition Prestel provide information about shopping opportunities and matters of local concern.

16.11 *Cable TV*

Although the advent of teleshopping is still remote, proposals are being made in this country for the development of cable TV which will provide opportunities for perceptive retailers. In the US trials are well on their way using one way and two way cables with a special converter and key pad for customer response.

16.12 *The transaction telephone*

In this country there are well over 13m credit cards in circulation. In order to contain the unit costs of processing customers' card based transactions it has been found necessary to modernise the system in areas such as:

(a) administrative costs;

(b) excessive spending;

(c) credit control;

(d) fraudulent use.

In the US transaction telephones are becoming commonplace in retail outlets and the system is being adopted here by a few large retailing outlets. Transaction telephones are similar in appearance to normal hand set receivers but in addition they have a small display module. Many have a card reader unit built into the telephone which provides a data telecommunications link between the retail outlet and the credit card company's computer centre.

16.13 *Computers in mail order management*

Initially computers were introduced to overcome a labour recruitment problem and were applied to areas such as:

(a) agency indexing;

(b) catalogue referencing;

(c) recording and monitoring the delivery, despatch and return of goods;

(d) sequential order picking,

By using a computer, the order can be fed directly into the system, via a VDU linked to the stock file. Orders can be immediately verified and, if the goods are available, the computer will print despatch notes and pass them on to the warehouse.

A simple computer program ensures that the various items from an order are sorted and printed out in the relevant despatch notes. This reduces the cost of staff and equipment and eliminates the need for the multiple order copies originally required.

16.14 *Computers in physical distribution management*

Computers are used extensively to improve depot efficiency in areas such as:

(a) the production of order documentation;
(b) the production of a sequential picking lists;
(c) recording stock levels;
(d) the control of stock movement;
(e) stock replenishment orders;
(f) the financial evaluation of stock;
(g) stock availability when orders are telephoned into the depot.

An increase in bulk picking will reduce labour costs and speed up the process of order compilation. If requirements can be bulk picked, then separated into individual orders, it will reduce the order picking cycle. To assist the process, a computer can:

(a) specify the optimum picking sequence;
(b) control the stock in picking locations;
(c) control the movement of equipment down narrow aisles;

In sophisticated storage and retrieval systems, the computer controls the allocation and transfer of pallets to storage locations and retrieves them in response to a data input order.

16.15 *Computers in the office*

Office technology has been slow to develop, however word processors are becoming more widely used, bringing with them developments such as:

(a) document transmission, i.e. electronic mail;
(b) world wide transmission to most types of equipment, e.g. Telex;
(c) home television/view data systems, e.g. Prestel.

The use of new equipment will require:

(a) improved keyboard skills;
(b) improved language skills;
(c) improved decision making;
(d) a desire to work with new technology;
(e) a wider knowledge of the business world.

The office worker of the future will have to think, solve problems, make decisions and be more accurate than at present.

16.16 *Customer accounting*

Computers can be readily converted to give a fully integrated accounting system by installing an accounting software package. These packages will transform a basically dumb machine into an intelligent unit that can correctly process every sale, purchase, nominal and VAT entry, in addition to:

(a) automatically updating relevant accounts;
(b) displaying/printing out every kind of report or analysis;
(c) automatically controlling incoming and outgoing invoices;
(d) monitoring credit levels and credit worthiness.

Most of the systems are easy to operate and require little technical or specialist knowledge. Some systems allow additional capacity to cater for future business expansion.

6.17 *Exercise 2*

1. Describe the scanning process.
2. Why is the article numbering of products important?
3. Where can portable computer data recording terminals be effectively used in distribution?
4. Explain the service provided by Prestel.
5. What is a transaction telephone and how does it differ from an ordinary telephone?
6. What impact have computers made in physical distribution management?

6.18 **Assignments**

1. Identify the effects of modern computer-based systems on the distributive trade.
2. Investigate the advantages and disadvantages connected with electronic fund transfer systems for both the retailer and the consumer.

Chapter 17

Advertising

At the end of this chapter you should be able to:-
(A) Explain the importance of promoting sales.
(B) Define advertising and identify its aims.
(C) Compare good and bad advertisements.
(D) List the functions of advertising.
(E) Describe the best advertising medium for a particular product or idea.
(F) List and identify the characteristics of the various advertising media.

17.1 *Sales promotion*

There are many reasons for promoting sales:-

(a) If a sales campaign is carefully prepared it can help a business become successful and remain so.

All businesses incur running expenses e.g. rent, rates, light or wages. A shop that can sell more goods for the same running expenses will have more profit left at the end of the year. See exhibit 17.01.

Running expenses for each shop are £15,000
Shop A sells £100,000 of goods per year at 25% gross profit
Shop B sells £160,000 of goods per year at 25% gross profit

Shop A		Shop B
£25,000	GROSS PROFIT	£40,000
£15,000	EXPENSES	£15,000
£10,000	NET PROFIT	£25,000

Exhibit 17.01
Relationship between Profit and Sales

(b) Many customers are not adventurous in their habits and constantly need reminding of new and interesting ideas, e.g. exotic foods or trendy fashions. This stimulates their desire for change and can lead to increased sales.

(c) There is constant pressure exerted on businessmen to expand. Some will use a large proportion of their profits to finance expansion if this is seen to be desirable. A diminishing turnover is seen by many to indicate a dying business. Do not forget that some shops sell only the same number of units each year. These are classed as static but survive in the face of competition provided they can keep up with inflation.

(d) Because of change in fashions, it is necessary to attract new customers, persuade them to discard their out-of-date clothes, and to buy new ones.

(e) People are continually moving in and out of an area due to changes in occupation, or the need to follow their employment. Older people retire or die and are replaced by younger ones with new ideas.

The newcomers must constantly be kept in touch with what is available for purchase.

(f) Customer loyalties can quickly change for many reasons, e.g. cheaper products, more choice or better services. Sales promotion can counteract these changes and be used by any business regardless of size or area.

17.2 *Advertising*

Advertising is any form of non personal presentation of goods, services, or even ideas, which is done by a particular person or company.

It must however follow certain steps in order to be successful:

(a) Catch attention;

(b) Arouse interest;

(c) Create desire;

(d) Induce action.

See Exhibits 17.02 and 17.03.

FRED'S
CROWN YARD

MENS PRE-SHRUNK POLYESTER/COTTON SHIRTS AT A SPECIAL PRICE OF £6-99 AVAILABLE IN THE FOLLOWING SIZES:- 14, 15, 16, 17, 18. PLENTY OF COLOURS TO CHOOSE FROM INCLUDING WHITE, BLUE, BROWN, GREEN, ORANGE AND PURPLE. IN PLAIN AND PATTERNED STYLES

Exhibit 17.01
Poor Advertisement

PAUL'S FASHIONS
TOWN HALL PARADE

MEN'S SHIRTS

ONLY

£6.99 each

ASSORTED SIZES, COLOURS AND STYLES

Exhibit 17.02
Good Advertisement

A well presented advertisement will give the maximum amount of impact. Care must be taken in the choice of layout, size, colour and message. The message must be straight and to the point, in type which is bold enough for the reader.

Advertisements must catch the eye as they are quickly passed over.

Once interest has been aroused the reader will stop and concentrate on what is written. Too many words will tend to dissuade readers as they search to pick out essential details. Specialist firms and advertising agencies can be usefully employed in any campaign.

17.3   *Aims of advertising*

Its main aims are to influence people's behaviour by encouraging them to:-

(a) Buy a certain product at the expense of similar ones already on the market e.g. food or detergents.

(b) Adopt some pattern of behaviour which is seen as socially desirable e.g. showing the dangers of not wearing a seatbelt, or asking drivers not to drink and drive.

17.4   *Functions of advertising*

(a) Its main function is to inform the public about new and different products on the market. In addition it gives information as to the uses of these products and where they can be bought.

(b) The public need constant persuasion as their memory is short. People forget very quickly, and the rate of forgetting increases as the time interval between reminders increases. One has only to watch an evenings TV to note the constant repetition which is applied in advertising.

(c) If an advertiser can sell more, then he can produce more. This allows his plant and machinery to be fully used and will reduce his costs per item. In turn this should give him more profit. See also 16.1(a).

17.5   *Exercise 1*

1. Imagine you are the owner of an advertising agency. Draft a handout which could be delivered to local retailers explaining why they should use your services.

17.6   *Choice of advertising media*

There are many types of advertising media. The one most suitable will depend on the market at which it is aimed e.g. children, teenagers, adults, smokers. The factors influencing the choice of medium include:-

(a) The social class and age group to whom the appeal is being made e.g. it would be a waste of time and money to advertise expensive jewellery in a magazine aimed at teenagers.

(b) National newspapers have a greater circulation than local newspapers and are aimed at a wider market. The product must have national appeal and be readily available if it is to sell in large quantities.

(c) One of the greatest problems with (b) above is that of cost in relation to the number of people 'reached'. Advertising rates in the national newspapers are extremely high in comparison with local rates, due to wider coverage.

17.7 Methods of advertising

There are many ways of advertising, some of which are given below:

(a) *Newspapers and magazines.*

These can be aimed at different sections of the community, from a simple three line advertisement in the classified columns of a local newspaper, to a full colour page in a popular magazine.

(b) *Television*

This is used by many organisations, and advertisements can be timed to reach a particular market e.g. fertilisers in farming programmes, or children's toys at tea time.

(c) *Radio*

Local commercial radio is becoming very popular and many items are advertised, including events such as galas, fayres and garden parties.

(d) *Outdoor*

Outdoor advertising consists of posters on hoardings, commercial vehicles, or buses, and illuminated signs, all of which perform a useful function. Strategically placed in large city centres, such advertising can be seen by thousands of people in a day.

(e) *Cinema*

Although cinema advertising is still very common it does not reach the same number of people it did twenty years ago, due to the drop in cinema attendances. It is mainly used by local firms.

(f) *Direct mail* (see also 6.8)

Another well used method of reaching the public is by direct mail. It ranges from one sheet of paper printed by a local shopkeeper promoting his goods, to the free samples and coupons sent out by major manufacturing companies e.g. shampoo, detergents, or coupons for new products. The local shopkeeper organises his own delivery, whilst the manufacturer usually employs a distributing agency.

(g) *Exhibitions and Fashion Parades*

These are organised by both retailers and manufacturers as a means of sales promotion. These are ideal methods of showing goods to a large proportion of the general public. Exhibitions can be incorporated in national events such as trade fairs where the exhibitor rents a site. At the other end of the scale are those organised on a local basis at, for example, an agricultural show. Fashion parades can be staged in large halls before an invited audience or on a small scale to finance a charity. See also 6.4 where goods are displayed and sold in the home.

(h) *Mail Order Catalogues.* See 6.6

(j) *Display.* See Chapter 18.

Advertising is expensive and many companies spend large amounts of money in persuading the public to buy their products. It must be remembered that the style of advertisement must match the style of product being advertised. Consideration must be given to seasonal changes or special events such as Mothers Day.

The money spent on advertising will be wasted if there is no back up promotion in the shop. It is essential that adequate displays are erected to tie in with the advertisement and its theme see 18.2(b). Ensure there is enough back up stock to avoid an out of stock position see 12.5. Above all it is the responsibility of senior management to ensure their staff are fully informed about current advertising. Most large organisations will distribute copies of advertisements prior to publication. These must be checked to ensure correct description and prices in order to avoid any legal action see 17.9 and 6.7(a)-(d).

7.8 Other ways of increasing sales

(a) Trading Stamps

Trading stamps are used by some shops as an inducement to buy goods or to maintain customer loyalty. The number of stamps given depends on how much the customer has spent. They can be exchanged for goods or cash, or used to obtain discount on goods.

(b) Special events

These take place throughout the year and consist of sales, promotions, special weeks or seasonal events. The shop can then clear old stock, promote new lines, and relate selling to events such as the Cup Tie or promoting goods from other countries.

(c) Word of mouth

This is a very important form of sales promotion and is often overlooked. It depends entirely on customer satisfaction and the way in which a customer has been treated in the store. Do not forget it can have the reverse effect if a dis-satisfied customer starts complaining to her friends.

7.9 Control of advertising

The standards of advertising in this country are already high due to the work of The Advertising Standards Authority. This is an independent body set up and paid for by the British advertising business. They protect the public from advertisers whose advertisements mislead, misrepresent or offend. Their work covers magazines, newspapers, cinema and direct mail advertising but not radio and TV. All advertising must be:-

(a) legal;

(b) decent;

(c) honest;

(d) truthful.

if it isn't it must be stopped. If any of these do not apply then any advertisement which breaks the Code of Advertising Practice (the 'rule book' governing British Advertising) are either corrected or withdrawn altogether. The ASA consider all complaints carefully, and publish lists naming advertisers involved in addition to setting out their decisions. The names of people who complain are never disclosed.

Television and radio advertising are much more closely controlled than any other form. This is because it takes place in the home and open to children of all ages. It is controlled by the Independent Broadcasting Authority in a similar way to press advertising. Many advertisement have been stopped on TV which were not considered to be in the public interest e.g. cigarettes. The Government can control advertising through the IBA but has not an independent body to review advertising from all sources.

17.10 *Exercise 2*

1. What factors would influence your choice of advertising medium?
2. List the various methods used in advertising.
3. What are trading stamps and why are they used?
4. Describe some methods other than advertising of promoting sales.
5. How is advertising controlled.

17.11 Assignments

1. Collect samples of printed advertisements and make notes on their effectiveness, coverage, and the age group at which they are aimed.
2. Design an advertisement suitable for either a newspaper or magazine using a product or article of your choice.

Chapter 18

Display

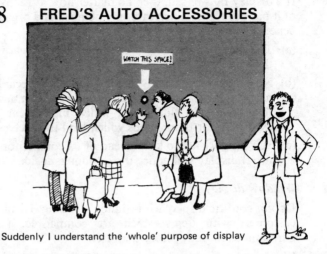

FRED'S AUTO ACCESSORIES

WATCH THIS SPACE!

Suddenly I understand the 'whole' purpose of display

At the end of his chapter you should be able to:-

(A) Explain the purposes of display.

(B) Appraise the benefits it can bring to a business.

(C) Distinguish between display and window dressing.

(D) Identify and illustrate the two types of display balance.

(E) Describe the characteristics of interior display.

(F) Explain the basic principles of colour and list some characteristics.

(G) Explain the need for lighting.

(H) Distinguish between tungsten and fluorescent lighting, their advantages and disadvantages.

(J) Explain the need for tickets in a display and identify problems in use.

18.1   Display plays an important part in promoting sales for the small shop, large store, or manufacturer. Its main purpose is to increase sales and also to show the general public merchandise a retailer wishes to promote. Display embraces many areas including:-

(a) windows;

(b) shop interiors;

(c) counter tops;

(d) special features.

In the main, the style of display varies with the size of retail outlet e.g. small trader, supermarket, or multiple. Each has its own distinctive image to promote.

124

18.2   If a display fails to sell, then no matter how attractive it is, the whole point of it has been lost. When carefully planned and organised it can bring many benefits to a business e.g.:

(a) The fact that a retailer uses display, helps to advertise his business and the type of goods he sells.

(b) New lines can readily be introduced especially when tied in with national advertising. This brings new life to a business and also helps to 'iron out' any fluctuation which may occur throughout the year, especially for those shops which lend themselves to seasonal trade.

(c) If a shop wishes to keep ahead of its competitors, then an attractive or novel display will entice the customers inside.

18.3   *Window display*

Do not confuse display with window dressing. Display is planned to attract customers with items which are compatible, tastefully set out and harmonious in both colour and use.

Window dressing tends to be overfilled with mixed items of merchandise covering the whole window area, usually indiscriminately placed, and sometimes bearing little relation to each other. It is not necessary to completely fill a window. Remember spaces are just as important as goods. Some windows are so full that the customer does not really see anything; a good example of this would be a seaside gift shop.

In order to look attractive a window must be well designed and above all balanced. There are two types of balance used in display:

(a) *Symmetrical,* where equal quantities in shape and amount are found on each side of a centre line drawn down the middle of a window. One half of the design reflects the other in every detail and produces a mirror image. See exhibit 18.01

(b) *Asymmetrical,* where the balance is visual and the items displayed have the appearance of balance in an arrangement which is pleasing to look at and complete in itself. See exhibit 18.02

18.4   *Shop interiors*

Every shop interior lends itself to display, whether it be corner shop, supermarket or large department store. Each has its own methods, but they all follow similar lines and meet the same requirements.

The display must complete the work of the window and have similar themes and characteristics. The large store will attract customers by their windows. Some link up is necessary inside the store to show prospective buyers where the goods are sold e.g. a display of luggage in the store will have a similar layout, colours, posters, and holiday theme, as that in the window. Supermarkets on the other hand use posters to attract customers by offering price reductions. These would need tying in with large displays of the same goods in special areas or at the end of aisles.

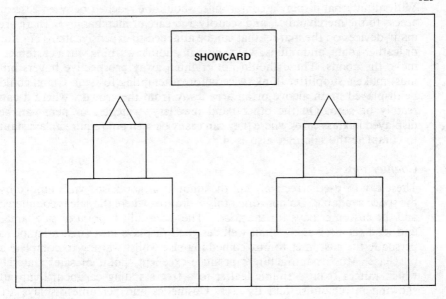

Exhibit 18.01
Symmetrical Balance

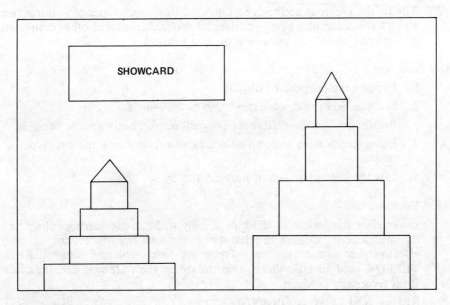

Exhibit 18.02
Asymmetrical Balance

126

With all internal display a compromise should be reached between ease of access to the merchandise, and security and care of merchandise. There are many devices on the market that can be attached to expensive items e.g. fur or leather coats, and radios, which give an audible warning when customers move the goods. These should not frighten away prospective buyers but must make a shoplifter think twice before attempting to steal. China could be displayed in an alcove or an area away from the crowds, where it can readily be seen. On the other hand jewellery, watches, or pens can be displayed in glass cases where they can easily be seen but require an assistant to complete the sale. See also 13.4

18.5   *Counter tops*

These can be used effectively but the amount of goods shown is limited by the space available. Do not forget this is the area where the sale is completed and the customer pays for the goods. These are called 'point of sale' areas and lend themselves to small well-designed displays in a final attempt to persuade the customer to buy something else whilst waiting to complete a purchase. Most manufacturers produce excellent 'point of sale' material which ranges from a simple leaflet to a free standing cardboard cut-out showing merchandise and its uses. Cosmetics and perfume displays are good examples of these, many of which can be obtained in varying sizes to suit the space available.

18.6   *Special features*

Any of the previous methods can be used to promote special features (see also 17.8(b) examples being continental foods, ideas from other countries, plus special stands, demonstrations, and tastings.

18.7   *Exercise 1*
1.   Explain the purpose of display.
2.   List the benefits display can bring to a business.
3.   Briefly explain the difference between display and window dressing.
4.   Using goods with which you are familiar, illustrate the two types of balance.
5.   List the characteristics of interior display.

18.8   *Colour*

It would be impossible to think of display without considering colour and its implications. Colour is what gives life and beauty. It can be used effectively to attract the eye. There are three primary colours, RED, YELLOW and BLUE, which when mixed in the following combinations form secondary colours:
RED + YELLOW = ORANGE
YELLOW + BLUE = GREEN
BLUE + RED = PURPLE

(a) The primary and secondary colours form the basic colour wheel as shown in the diagram. See exhibit 18.03

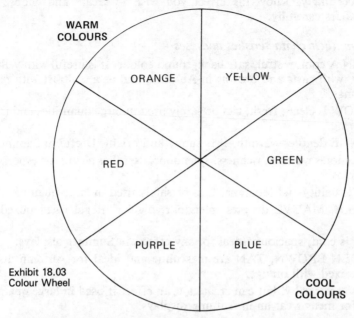

Exhibit 18.03
Colour Wheel

(b) Contrasting or complementary colours are those directly opposite each other in the colour wheel e.g. red and green.

(c) Harmonising or analogous colours are those close to each other on the wheel e.g. red and organge.

Contrasting colours are striking but should not be used in equal amounts.

(d) Blends are tasteful and restful. Two colours or shades of one colour create the best schemes. Pastel colours are easiest to mix. Colours should be in character with the merchandise. More dominant colours or contrasts should be used to draw attention. Balance can be seriously affected by colour. A perfectly balanced display can be disturbed by the wrong colour combination, whereas a scheme slightly out of balance can be corrected e.g. a small area of a strong colour will be balanced by a larger area of lighter colour.

(e) Warm colours tend to bring articles forward and cool colours tend to make articles recede. This can be put to good use e.g. by painting a small window blue it would appear more spacious. Many students complain that they cannot appreciate colour. One way to overcome this problem is to follow Nature which blends colours correctly. Note the harmonious blend of green and yellow in Spring daffodils and the contrasting red berries in a bush of green holly. The natural order of colours can be seen in the ripening of a plum which starts with a green skin then follows through yellow, orange, red, and finally purple.

(f) Many of the hard and fast rules about the use of colour have now gone. It is far better to be aware of the colour trends of the day and use them accordingly. Know the effect you wish to create and choose your colours carefully.

18.9 *Colours, their characteristics and uses*

GREEN A cool, restful, safe background colour. It is useful with yellow in Spring, with rusts and browns in Autumn, and as a contrast with red for Christmas.

YELLOW is clean, fresh, can be safely used in large quantities and is ideal for Spring.

ORANGE denotes warmth. It is sunny and bright. Useful in Summer.

RED denotes warmth, richness, splendour, useful as a contrast especially at Christmas.

PINK is dainty and feminine. Can be safely used in large quantities.

PURPLE, MAUVE denotes splendour, dignity. Regal when mixed with gold.

BLUE is cold, spacious. Ideal for sky effects in Summer displays.

GOLDEN BROWN, TAN are masculine and ideal for Autumn displays when mixed with orange.

BROWN is earthy, but can create a drab effect if used in large quantities. Ideal for mens wear an in Autumn displays.

18.10 *Exercise 2*

1. Why is colour essential to display?
2. Give examples of primary and secondary colours.
3. Which colours are used in the basic colour wheel and in what order do they follow each other?
4. Give examples of warm and cool colours.
5. In a rectangle 12 cm × 20 cm draw an abstract design to illustrate either complementary or harmonious colours.

18.11 *Lighting*

Lighting of displays is very important and should be given a great deal of thought. It is used for:-

(a) illumination;

(b) effect.

There are two main types used:-

(a) tungsten, i.e. using bulbs in reflectors or spotlights;

(b) fluorescent, i.e. tubular.

Each has its own advantages and disadvantages. See exhibit 18.04

TUNGSTEN	FLUORESCENT
Advantages	*Advantages*
1. No danger of colour distortion	1. Less expensive to run
2. Less expensive to install	2. Less heat generated in use
3. Ideal for spotlighting	
4. Used for flashing coloured lights	
5. Flexible when combined with track systems	
Disadvantages	*Disadvantages*
1. Very hot, especially spotlights	1. Expensive to install
2. Expensive to run	2. Can cause colour distortion
	3. Correct shade for goods must be used

A good lighting system should be very flexible ranging from flooding a large area to spotlighting small objects. It will consist of banks of fluorescent tubes backed up with tungsten 'spots'. Movement can be brought in by using lights shining through revolving coloured oils and patterns.

18.12 *Ticketing*

Good show cards and price tickets are essential to increase the selling potential of a display. They must be legible, brief, and to the point so that a short sharp message can be given to the customer. (See exhibits 17.02 and 17.03)

Make sure they are placed where they can easily be read without hiding any merchandise. Too many tickets should be avoided as they tend to distract the customer. Size of ticket varies with individual taste and merchandise. make sure they are neither too large or too small for the display. Many unusual tickets can be made or found and add interest to a display, especially if they can be related to it e.g. pebbles or sea shells in a holiday or swimwear display. Other examples which have been used are; flower pots, bricks, eggs, small flags, playing cards and luggage labels. When the display has been completed, look at it from the same position as the customer i.e. from outside. Many mistakes will be quickly spotted e.g. poor lighting effects, spotlights not focussed correctly, showcard hiding some of the merchandise, and even finger marks on glass or mirrors. Do not be afraid to make adjustments at this stage. It may be advantageous to remove an item rather than create an overfilled or unbalanced effect. Good effective display can certainly enhance a business and attract more customers. Do not be afraid to experiment or use novel ideas regardless of general opinion. At all times it is better to be original than adopt other peoples ideas.

18.13 *Exercise 3*

1. For what purpose is lighting used in display?
2. What is the difference between tungsten and fluorescent lighting?
3. List the advantages and disadvantages of both forms of lighting.
4. Design an unusual ticket which will add interest to a display, using merchandise of your own choice.

18.14 Assignments

1. Choose two stores and compare them with the check list given. Be prepared to substantiate any statements you make. At the end of the survey make suggestions for improving the overall appearance of each.

2. Construct a colour wheel, and colour each section correctly. On it mark a cross to show two complementary colours, and mark two analogous colours with a tick. Distinguish between the cool and warm colours.

Index